WORKBOOK TO ACCOMPANY
Writing & Reporting
FOR THE MEDIA

WORKBOOK TO ACCOMPANY
Writing & Reporting
FOR THE MEDIA

TWELFTH EDITION

JOHN R. BENDER
UNIVERSITY OF NEBRASKA-LINCOLN

LUCINDA D. DAVENPORT
MICHIGAN STATE UNIVERSITY

MICHAEL W. DRAGER
SHIPPENSBURG UNIVERSITY OF PENNSYLVANIA

FRED FEDLER
UNIVERSITY OF CENTRAL FLORIDA

NEW YORK | OXFORD
OXFORD UNIVERSITY PRESS

Oxford University Press is a department of the University of Oxford.
It furthers the University's objective of excellence in research, scholarship,
and education by publishing worldwide. Oxford is a registered trade mark of
Oxford University Press in the UK and certain other countries.

Published in the United States of America by Oxford University Press
198 Madison Avenue, New York, NY 10016, United States of America.

© 2019, 2016, 2012, 2009, 2005 by Oxford University Press

CONTENTS

Name _____ **Class** _____ **Date** _____

EXERCISE TO ACCOMPANY CHAPTER 1

Journalism Today

Introduction

This workbook has been designed to accompany *Writing & Reporting for the Media*'s 12th edition in order to provide extra practice for students. The exercises in this workbook ask you to become more familiar with journalism practices, various grammatical rules and style organization, as well as help you to think more about what it really means to be a journalist in our time. Some of these exercises will be sentence corrections and rewrites, while other exercises will ask you to take on a slightly larger and more in-depth project. With the ever increasing amount of information available at the touch of a button, it's important to understand what we read and be able to assess it critically for validity, audience and quality writing.

EXERCISES: Getting Started

What piques your interest in journalism? What do you hope to learn from this course?

List three journalism-focused goals you will set for yourself to achieve by the end of this course.

1.

2.

3.

Describe the way you interact with the news on a daily basis.

Name _____   Class _____   Date _____

EXERCISES TO ACCOMPANY CHAPTER 2

Selecting and Reporting the News

EXERCISE 1: Discussion Questions

INSTRUCTIONS: Read the questions below and discuss them with your instructor and your classmates. Try to consider the questions from several vantage points—as the editor, as the reporter and as the audience reading the story. Consider, too, how your decisions might change for different audiences and whether you are publishing in print, online or over the air.

1. Normally, newspapers report every birth, death, divorce and bankruptcy in their community.

   A. Do you agree with that policy? Why?

   B. As editor, would you include the births to unwed mothers?

2. As editor, would you also report every local suicide? Why?

3. As editor of your local daily, you normally avoid cheesecake: pictures of scantily clad young women. But a student on your campus won the Miss America preliminaries in your state and has flown to Atlantic City for the national finals. During the first day of competition there, your paper received only one photograph, and it shows her and two other contestants in bikinis at a beach. Would you publish the photograph? Why?

4. Assume that your mayor has often criticized the city's welfare system and the fact that some recipients are able-bodied adults, without children. If you learned that your mayor's 27-year-old son (who does not live at home) was broke because of a business failure and was applying for welfare, would you publish the story?

5. Assume that three local high school students, each 15 years old, have been charged with arson; they started a fire that caused $80,000 in damage at their high school, closing it for a day.

   A. If you obtained the students' names, and it was legal to do so, would you identify them in your story?

   B. Before publishing the story, would you call and warn (or interview) the students or their parents?

6. Reporters are forced to make difficult decisions about what elements of a story are most newsworthy. Assume that, earlier today, two men robbed a local restaurant and shot a customer. Then, during a high-speed chase through the city, a police car skidded out of control and struck a pedestrian, a 34-year-old nurse. Both the customer and the pedestrian have been hospitalized in serious condition. Which element would you

Name _____ Class _____ Date _____

emphasize in the first paragraph of your story, known as the lead: the customer shot by two robbers or the pedestrian struck by police chasing the robbers?

7. If a member of the American Nazi Party spoke in your community and criticized blacks, Jews and immigrants, would you report the story? How could you justify the story's publication or suppression?

8. Imagine that a member of your city council, a Democrat, offered to give you information proving that store personnel had caught your mayor, a Republican, shoplifting. The store's owner declined to prosecute. Moreover, the Democrat insists that you keep his identity a secret: that you never identify your source. The Democrat is a potential candidate for mayor: an obvious rival. Yet the information is accurate. How would you respond?

9. Assume that a local woman today announced her candidacy for mayor. Which—if any—of these facts about her personal life would you include in a story about her candidacy?

    A. She is 57 years old.

    B. She is a millionaire.

    C. She is the mother of four children.

    D. She is 5 feet 1 inch tall, has gray hair, and weighs 180 pounds.

    E. Her first husband died, and she divorced her second.

    F. Her first husband committed suicide two years after their marriage.

    G. After her husband's death, she transformed a small restaurant they established into one of the largest and finest in the city.

    H. She now lives with a bank executive.

    I. The bank executive is 36 years old.

    J. One of her sons is a high school teacher. Two help her in the restaurant. The fourth is in prison, convicted of selling cocaine.

10. Which of the details you want to publish about the candidate described in Question 9 would affect her performance if she was elected mayor?

    A. If some of the details about her private life would not affect her performance as mayor, how can you justify their publication?

    B. Would you publish the same details about a male candidate?

EXERCISE 2: Discussion Questions

INSTRUCTIONS: Read the questions below and discuss them with your instructor and your classmates. Try to consider the questions from several vantage points—as the editor, as the reporter and as the audience reading the story.

Name _____   **Class** _____   **Date** _____

1. What do you think is "news"? Can you devise a good definition of the term?

2. Do you agree with a number of media critics, who believe that the media report too much bad news? If so, how would you correct the problem?

3. Some have criticized many local news broadcasts as placing too much emphasis on crime and death.

   A. Do you think that the critics are right: that local newscasts devote too much time to crime and violence?

   B. If so, why do you think that local newscasts devote so much time to that type of story?

   C. Is the public inconsistent? Many Americans complain that the media report too much bad news. But would television stations broadcast that type of story if the public didn't like it: that is, if the stories didn't help boost the stations' ratings?

4. Imagine that you edited your local daily. Would you print the racist and sexist lyrics sung by a controversial rap musician? Why?

5. Imagine that you edited your local daily. How would you report on an exhibition in a local art museum that featured a collection of photographs that included homoerotic images of nude men engaged in various sex acts? How specifically would you have described the photographs?

6. Should newspapers devote more space to worthwhile causes and organizations in their communities, recognizing and promoting their good work?

7. While working for a newspaper—or any other medium—have you encountered any "sacred cows": policies that reflected the interests (or prejudices) of your editor or publisher?

8. Do you believe that journalists are objective? If not, would you want them to abandon the concept of objectivity? Why?

9. Do you read your local daily either in print or online? Why?

   A. If you don't, is there anything that its editor could do to improve the paper so that you would read it?

   B. If you (or a classmate) said you do not have time to read a daily newspaper, do you also lack the time to watch television?

   C. If editors fail to interest young adults in reading newspapers, will that generation of Americans ever begin to read a paper? If not, how can newspapers survive?

10. A recent study concluded that young adults "know less and care less about news and public affairs than any other generation of Americans in the past 50 years?" Do you believe that conclusion is an accurate one? Why?

11. Do you agree with the statements that (1) newspapers are obsolete and that (2) reading newspapers is an old people's habit? Why?

Name _____   Class _____   Date _____

EXERCISE 3: News Judgment

INSTRUCTIONS: The decisions journalists make every day are difficult, involving matters of importance, interest, taste, ethics and myriad other considerations. The following questions ask you to make those types of decisions. After deciding which stories to use and emphasize, compare your decisions with those of your classmates.

1. Imagine that, on the same day, the president of the United States presents his annual State of the Union message and the jury in the criminal trial of a major Hollywood movie star for murdering his wife announces its verdict. During his speech, the president proposes raising the hourly minimum wage $3. Which of the two stories would you place at the top of Page 1?

2. As editor of your local daily newspaper, you have space for one more photograph on Page 1. Circle the photograph from the following list that you would select.

    A. A photograph showing 32 members of a local high school choir leaving to sing at a prestigious festival in Vienna.

    B. A photograph showing a car torn in half by a train at a crossing in your city, killing the driver and her five young children.

    C. A photograph showing a graduate of your college who won a Fulbright Scholarship to spend a year studying at Cambridge, England. While using a wheelchair, the student earned all A's and was president of your Student Senate.

    D. A photograph showing a computer hacker who today pleaded guilty to entering your college's computer system and changing the grades of more than 100 other students, mostly members of a few fraternities and sororities. The hacker charged $250 to change a grade, and school officials say it will take months and cost $50,000 or more for them to verify every grade recorded in the past two years.

    E. A photograph showing actor Jennifer Lawrence visiting a brother who lives in your city.

    F. A photograph showing dozens of children who are sick, hungry, poorly clothed and lying—and dying—outside an aid station: victims of one of the most severe droughts in African history.

3. Rank these nine stories by their newsworthiness, starting with "1" for the most newsworthy:

    A. _____A local businessman today donated $12 million to construct a YMCA in your community.

    B. _____Your mayor today admitted that she is an alcoholic and is committing herself to a six-week residential treatment program—but will not resign.

    C. _____Your city's Economic Development Board today revealed that a major pharmaceutical company will open a plant in an industrial park in your city and hire 400 people.

Name _____   **Class** _____   **Date** _____

D. _____A thunderstorm struck your city at about 6 this morning, dropping 1.7 inches of rain. Wind gusts exceeding 40 mph blew down dozens of trees and left thousands of people without power.

E. _____Actor Shia LaBeouf was arrested today for public intoxication and disturbing the peace.

F. _____An Indian airliner crashed while trying to land at New Delhi's airport during a thunderstorm, killing all 230 people on board.

G. _____A three-alarm fire in an apartment complex in your city destroyed 12 units, leaving their residents homeless and two firefighters slightly injured.

H. _____Your city's police department today settled a bias suit filed by eight current and former police officers, all women. The city agreed to pay $540,000 to be divided equally among the women, who said that because of their gender they were never promoted.

I. _____A busboy at a popular restaurant in your city has been diagnosed with tuberculosis, and health officials advise thousands of people who ate at the restaurant to be tested for the infectious disease.

4. Rank these nine stories by their newsworthiness, starting with "1" for the most newsworthy:

A. _____The largest church in your city today announced plans to develop a new campus that will eventually include six buildings: a church, a social hall, a day care center, an elementary school, a three-story home for the elderly and a recreational center for teens.

B. _____Officials at a local community college today learned that the college has won a $7.6 million federal grant to provide job training for welfare recipients. The program is expected to serve about 240 people a year for five years.

C. _____A leading stock car racer was killed last night in a car accident on a highway near his home.

D. _____Someone bombed an abortion clinic in Chicago last night, causing $100,000 in damage.

E. _____Emma Watson today announced that she is getting married and quitting acting to start a family.

F. _____The president's wife will fly to your city and visit an elementary school with an innovative program for teaching foreign languages.

G. _____The stock market rose 2.8 percent yesterday, reaching a record high.

H. _____After years of debate, residents of Puerto Rico voted by a margin of 52–48 percent to become a state.

I. _____A new federal study has found that when a car collides with a larger pickup truck or sport utility vehicle, the driver of the car is 30 times more likely than the driver of the larger vehicle to be killed.

Name _____   **Class** _____   **Date** _____

5. Normally, your newspaper does not report rumors. Mark any cases in which you would make an exception.

   A. _____ Because of his success at your college during the past eight years, your football coach is reportedly being offered the top job at Notre Dame.

   B. _____ One of your city's largest employers is reportedly closing its manufacturing plant and moving to Mexico, terminating all 400 of its local jobs.

   C. _____ A popular and upscale department store—Saks Fifth Avenue—is reportedly considering a downtown site in your city.

   D. _____ During the past three months, four babies born at Mercy Hospital in your city have died. All were apparently healthy at birth. Hospital and state medical experts are reportedly investigating the existence of a deadly infection.

   E. _____ A popular anchorman on the top-rated local newscast in your city has reportedly been offered—and has accepted—a job in Los Angeles.

6. If a 15-year-old boy in your community was charged with killing his mother and stepfather, which of these details would you include in your story and which would you discard?

   A. _____ The boy was an Eagle Scout.

   B. _____ The boy had twice run away from home and twice been arrested by police.

   C. _____ The boy never knew his father, a construction worker who disappeared shortly after his birth.

   D. _____ The boy told friends that he hated his stepfather.

   E. _____ Friends said the boy shoplifted, usually beer, and was sometimes drunk.

   F. _____ Friends said they thought, but were not certain, the stepfather beat the boy, since while swimming they noticed bruises the boy refused to explain.

   G. _____ The boy was 60 to 80 pounds overweight and a poor athlete.

   H. _____ Psychoanalyzing him, an English teacher who knew the boy said he seemed to be full of hostility he tried to repress.

   I. _____ Social workers investigated—but were unable to substantiate—suspicions that the boy was sexually molested by an uncle.

7. Patricia Richards, a 52-year-old business woman in your city, today announced that she is running for mayor. You know and can prove all the following facts but have never reported them because she was a private citizen. Mark the facts you would report today.

   A. _____ Richards has been divorced three times.

   B. _____ At the age of 17, Richards and two friends were charged with stealing a car. The charges were dropped because the car was recovered undamaged and the car's owner, a neighbor, declined to prosecute.

   C. _____ Richards has diabetes.

D. _____Richards has had two abortions.

E. _____Richards is a recovered alcoholic; she has not had a drink in 20 years.

F. _____Before going into business for herself, she was fired from two other jobs because of her drinking.

G. _____Her campaign literature says she attended the University of Iowa, yet she never graduated.

H. _____She established, owns and manages the city's largest chain of furniture stores.

I. _____Various tax and other public records reveal that her chain of furniture stores is valued at $20 million and last year earned a profit of $2.3 million.

J. _____Each year, Richards donates more than $1 million to local charities that help troubled young women, but she always avoids publicity, insisting that the charities never mention her donations.

Name _____   Class _____   Date _____

Newswriting Style

EXERCISE 1: Avoiding Sexism

SECTION I: AVOIDING SEXIST TITLES

INSTRUCTIONS: Replace these titles with words that include both men and women.

1. Businessman
2. Chairman
3. Congressman
4. Craftsman
5. Fatherland
6. Fatherly
7. Founding Fathers
8. Man
9. Mankind
10. Man-sized
11. Paperboy
12. Repairman
13. Salesman
14. Statesman
15. Workman

SECTION II: AVOIDING MALE NOUNS AND PRONOUNS

INSTRUCTIONS: Rewrite the following sentences, eliminating their use of male nouns and pronouns.

1. A reporter is expected to protect his sources.

2. A good athlete often jogs to build his endurance.

3. Normally, every auto mechanic buys his own tools.

4. No one knows which of the nation's congressmen leaked the details to his wife and friends.

5. If a patient is clearly dying of cancer, doctors may give him enough drugs to ease his pain, and perhaps even enough to hasten his death.

SECTION III: AVOIDING STEREOTYPES

INSTRUCTIONS: Rewrite the following sentences, avoiding sexist language and comments.

1. Randy Ortiz married his wife seven years ago.

2. Tom Yapengco and his wife urged their son, James, to act like a man.

3. A male nurse, Richard Diaz, and his wife, an authoress, arrived today.

4. Lois Zarrrinfar, who never married, is 73 and the daughter of a famous poetess.

5. The bank's chairman said that the average depositor has $3,248 in his savings account.

Name _____   Class _____   Date _____

6. The two married ladies, both trim redheads, are serving as the program co-chairmen.

7. The city fathers announced that 10 men and 4 females, all clergymen, will serve on the board.

8. The store sells toys of all types, from guns and chemistry sets for boys to dolls and beauty kits for girls.

9. Although a wife and the mother of four, Mrs. Henry Conaho, a slender blonde, is also president of the community college.

10. A spokesman for the company announced that it has reached a gentleman's agreement with the sportsmen on their use of the woods.

EXERCISE 2: Being Concise

SECTION I: USING SIMPLE WORDS

INSTRUCTIONS: Substitute simpler and more common words for each of these words.

1. altercation
2. assistance
3. apprehend
4. attempt
5. commence

6. community
7. incarcerate
8. intoxicated
9. lacerations
10. ordinance

11. purchase
12. reimburse
13. relocate
14. request
15. residence

SECTION II: AVOIDING REDUNDANT PHRASES

INSTRUCTIONS: The following phrases do not have to be rewritten: simply cross off their unnecessary words.

1. are in need of
2. are now
3. are presently
4. brilliant genius
5. first discovered

6. future plans
7. hanged to death
8. head up
9. honest truth
10. in an effort to

11. is presently
12. now costs
13. seek to find
14. totally destroyed
15. whether or not

SECTION III: AVOIDING WORDY PHRASES

INSTRUCTIONS: Use a single word to replace each of these phrases.

1. absence of danger

2. are in agreement

3. at present

4. gave chase to

5. gave their approval

Name _____   Class _____   Date _____

6. get underway

7. in the course of

8. is hopeful that

9. made the ruling

10. made their escape

11. made a contribution

12. made their exit

13. posed a question

14. proceeded to leave

15. a short distance away

SECTION IV: ELIMINATING UNNECESSARY WORDS

INSTRUCTIONS: Eliminate the unnecessary words from the following sentences. The sentences do not have to be rewritten; simply cross off the words that are not needed.

1. Anyone may participate if they would like to.

2. Before the robbers left, they also took some liquor.

3. At the present time, about 100 students participate.

4. The results showed that only 31 percent passed the test.

5. Firefighters reached the scene and extinguished the blaze.

SECTION V: REWRITING WORDY SENTENCES

INSTRUCTIONS: Rewrite the following sentences, eliminating as many words as possible.

1. He said the cost of putting on the program will be about $500.

2. The police officer opened fire, shooting six times at the suspect.

3. Sanchez was taken to Memorial Hospital and is in fair condition there.

4. They told the midwife that there was not much time left before the baby was due.

5. Of the 10 stock car drivers interviewed, 8 felt like it is inevitable that you are going to have some injuries and deaths among the people participating in their races.

Name _____   Class _____   Date _____

SECTION VI: SIMPLIFYING OVERLOADED SENTENCES

INSTRUCTIONS: The following sentences are too long and complicated. Divide them into simpler, more concise sentences.

1. Two high school students, Joan Harnish and Sara Courhesne, were driving north on Carpenter Road at 10:20 p.m. when they came around a sharp curve in the road and noticed a wrecked motorcycle and, about 25 feet away, a man, about 20 years of age—apparently seriously injured—sprawled near a telephone pole.

2. In a 122-page report, the Department of Health and Human Services stated that drunken driving causes 28,000 traffic deaths a year, costing the nation $45 billion, and that nearly 9 million persons suffer from alcoholism or lesser drinking problems, a number that represents 10 percent of the U.S. workforce.

3. A Colonial High School student, Cynthia Allersen, who was driving the car, a teacher's new Buick, was taking four other high school students, including three exchange students from Germany, to a nearby shopping mall when another car smashed broadside into her vehicle at the intersection of Polle Street and Fuller Road, seriously injuring two of the exchange students.

EXERCISE 3: Testing All Your Skills

SECTION I: AVOIDING REDUNDANT PHRASES

INSTRUCTIONS: The following phrases are redundant. They do not have to be rewritten: simply cross off the unnecessary words.

1. brand new	6. jail facility	11. right now
2. combine together	7. join together	12. small in size
3. continue on	8. new discovery	13. true facts
4. crowd of people	9. past experience	14. unpaid debt
5. foreign imports	10. personal friend	15. won a victory

SECTION II: AVOIDING SEXUAL STEREOTYPES

INSTRUCTIONS: Rewrite the following sentences, avoiding sexist language and comments.

1. A California man and his wife attended the reunion.

2. The bus driver, a divorced lady, was blamed for the accident.

3. While the girls were playing tennis, their husbands were playing golf.

4. While her husband works, Valerie Dawkins raises their children and dabbles in politics.

5. Mrs. John Favata is a widow, 56 years old and a petite grandmother but still plays tennis five days a week and, today, won the city's Senior Women's Tournament.

SECTION III: REMAINING OBJECTIVE

INSTRUCTIONS: The following sentences do not have to be rewritten. Simply cross off the opinionated words and phrases.

1. Only 7 of the 94 people aboard the ill-fated plane were killed.

2. The boy's grief-stricken father says he intends to sue the prestigious school.

3. In an important speech Monday, the governor said the state must adopt needed laws to protect the unfortunate victims.

4. Eighty-six students miraculously escaped injury when an alert pedestrian noticed the flames and quickly warned them to leave.

5. One of the most interesting facts he revealed was that the Chinese replace each barrel of oil with one barrel of water to ensure that all their oil is pumped out of the ground.

SECTION IV: ELIMINATING UNNECESSARY WORDS

INSTRUCTIONS: Eliminate the unnecessary words from the following sentences. The sentences do not have to be rewritten; simply cross off the unnecessary words.

1. Since the inception of the program, it has saved three lives.

2. The boy was submerged under the water for about five minutes.

3. He was pinned in the car for 40 minutes before he could be removed.

4. The engineer said that, in her opinion, relatively few people actually use the road.

5. The center will have a total of eight separate offices for different ministers to occupy.

SECTION V: AVOIDING WORDY PHRASES

INSTRUCTIONS: Substitute a single word for the wordy phrases in the following sentences.

1. The gunman made off with about $700.

2. Her medical bills are in excess of $35,000.

3. The operation left him in a state of paralysis.

4. The new law will no longer allow tinted car windows.

5. Margaret Van Den Shruck addressed her speech to the Rotary Club.

Name _____ Class _____ Date _____

SECTION VI: SIMPLIFYING SENTENCES

INSTRUCTIONS: Rewrite the following sentences more simply and clearly.

1. He was the recipient of numerous awards and honors.

2. The police were then summoned to the park by a girl.

3. She said that their farm is in close proximity to the park.

4. Snow-removal vehicles are undertaking a cleanup of the city.

5. They said that a visit to their grandmother's was where they were going.

SECTION VII: TESTING ALL YOUR SKILLS

INSTRUCTIONS: Rewrite the following sentences, correcting all their errors.

1. They reached a settlement of the debt.

2. Applications must be submitted on or before the deadline date of March 1.

3. A total of eight qualified persons, four men and four females, served on the important committee.

4. They mayor said that, at the present time, she is favorably disposed towards the passage of the important new law.

5. When questioned by the police, the suspect, an unidentified juvenile, maintained that he had been drinking and had no recollection at all of the events that transpired on that tragic Saturday night in question.

EXERCISE 4: Testing All Your Skills

SECTION I: AVOIDING REDUNDANT PHRASES

INSTRUCTIONS: The following phrases are redundant. They do not have to be rewritten. Simply cross off the unnecessary words.

1. at a later date	6. future goals	11. referred back to
2. abolish altogether	7. hanged down from	12. sent away for
3. are currently	8. in order for	13. set a new record
4. first became	9. mental anguish	14. sum of $600
5. free of charge	10. personal habit	15. They both agreed

SECTION II: AVOIDING WORDY PHRASES

INSTRUCTIONS: Use a single word to replace each of these phrases.

1. adversely affected	4. caused injuries to	7. is in need of
2. came to a halt	5. free of wordiness	8. proceeded to go
3. caused damage to	6. in advance of	9. were aware of

Name _____   Class _____   Date _____

SECTION III: AVOIDING SEXUAL STEREOTYPES

INSTRUCTIONS: Rewrite the following sentences, eliminating their sexist language and comments.

1. Mike Deacosta, his wife and their two children, Mark and Amy, served as the hosts.

2. Councilman Alice Cycler, the attractive wife of a lawyer and mother of eight girls, is fighting to improve the city's parks.

3. In addition to raising their four children and caring for their home, Nikki Evans has also succeeded as a banker. Today she was promoted to vice president.

4. An attractive young blonde, Elaine Gardepe, seems to be an unlikely person to write a book about the topic, yet her book about auto mechanics has become a best seller.

5. She is a quiet woman, but the 52-year-old divorcee has a reputation for being an aggressive competitor. Last year she sold more homes than any other salesman in the city.

SECTION IV: REMAINING OBJECTIVE

INSTRUCTIONS: Rewrite the following sentences, eliminating their expressions of opinion.

1. Rudely, the two sullen-looking boys got up and left.

2. His provocative speech was well received, as he was interrupted 17 times by applause.

3. They announced that residents of the city can look forward to the construction of a beautiful new $4.1 million library next year.

4. Another important concept is the author's startling idea that it does not matter whether children begin to read before they are 10 years old.

5. It should be kept in mind, however, that with the interstate highway only 5 miles away, the facility is easily accessible to all the residents of the state.

SECTION V: AVOIDING UNNECESSARY WORDS

INSTRUCTIONS: Delete the unnecessary words from the following sentences; do not rewrite the sentences.

1. He is currently serving time in prison.

2. The men were in the process of painting a house when they fell.

3. What the group opposed was legislation that would totally ban nudity.

4. The university is currently in the process of building a new stadium.

5. They said that a major problem with the program is that it is now too expensive.

SECTION VI: SIMPLIFYING SENTENCES

INSTRUCTIONS: Rewrite the following sentences as clearly and simply as possible.

1. They fear that its effects may be detrimental.

2. They extended an invitation to her to join their sorority.

3. Anonymous sources are perceived as unreliable by the public.

4. The enclosed resume will give you an idea of my training and experience.

5. Another person who saw what was happening said the arrests will serve as a deterrent to other lawless criminals.

SECTION VII: SIMPLIFYING OVERLOADED SENTENCES

INSTRUCTIONS: Rewrite each of the following sentences, dividing them into shorter, simpler sentences.

1. The injured boy was taken to Mercy Hospital where a spokesman said the youth, who is from Seattle, Washington, was in serious condition with a gunshot wound to the chest accidentally fired by a friend with a .22 caliber revolver they found in a box.

2. The man, described by witnesses as about 30, slender, white and bald, leaped from a blue Ford car at about 3 p.m., grabbed a vinyl bag being carried by Max Butler, then shot him three times, fatally wounding him, before escaping with the bag that contained an estimated $10,000 that Butler, a courier for the First National Bank, had picked up from a realtor.

3. The chase, which reached speeds of 80 miles an hour, ended when the Pontiac struck two other cars on Holton Drive, where the police arrested the Pontiac's driver, identified as Lynn R. Pryor, and charged her with armed robbery, reckless driving and fleeing to elude capture following an incident in which a convenience store on Mercy Drive was robbed of less than $20 shortly after 6 a.m. this morning.

EXERCISE 5: Format

INSTRUCTIONS: Edit the following news stories to conform to Associated Press style and to correct any errors of spelling, punctuation and grammar.

```
Girl Scouts
      the countys Girl Scout Council no loonger will acept any checks during
its annual cookie sale-a-thon.
      During its last sale-a-thon, the council lost $4,284 due to worthlesschecks.
```

Name _____ Class _____ Date _____

"That may not sound like a lot, but its a serious loss for us," said Linda Goree, the Girl Scout county executive. "It cuts into our profits, but al so wastes too many hours of our timme."

Next year, Goree said, thecountys Girl Scouts will accept only cash

Two factors agravated the prov problem during the scouts last sale-a-thon, Goree continued. first, more pepople paid by check. Second, a larger percentage of the checks teh Girl Scouts received bounced.

"Some people pay by check beause they don't have the cash," Goree said. "Or, they want to place a large order. We have people who place orders for $100 or more, and thosse poeple are especially likely to pay by check.   we also receive checks for a little as one or two dollars."

Scout leaders call people who signed the checks that bounce and, in most cases,ask them to mail neW checks to the cty. office. The scout leadesr are unable to reach everyone, however. Smoe People have moved. Other s do not have telephones -- or do not seem to answer their tele phones.

"usually its an honest mistake, ad andpeople are embarrassed when we call them," Goree said. "THey want to take care of the problem right away.   Other people say they want to pay but dont have the money, and

we can usually work something out with them. Unfortunately, there are other people who get mad at us, like its our fault or something, and refuse to pay. Or, they write new checks that also bounce. It puts our leadess in a terrible situaton. A Girl Scout leadershouldn't have to deal with problems like that. Also, its not a good situation or example for our girls, and that's the reason for our ne w policy, why we'll

no longer accept any checks."

###

Men's Longevity

Being a middle-aged man and single can be deadly, too sociologists at your college warned today

Name _____   **Class** _____   **Date** _____

The sociologists, Margo Matos and LeeAnne verkler, found that middle-aged men who remain single double their chances of dying.

For 10 years, Matos and verkler tracked one thoussand men in the state. All of the men were 40 old years at the start of the study, and half were married. Matos and Verkler fuond that 11.7 percent of the men who remained unmarried died before their 50th birthday, compared to only 5.9 percent of themen who remained married.

Some of the maried men were divorced or widowed during the study, and 7.1 percnt of those who remainedd alone for at least half the period also died.

"We arent sure of all the reasons," verkler said. "That's what we'll look at next. WE think poor diet plays a role. Also the use of alcohol, smoking, a lack of exercise and low incomes. Men who live by themselves seem to do more drinking and smoking, and many don't PREprepare good meals for them-selves. Plus there's the absence of social support. It ehlps to have someone to talk with, someone who shpares your li fe and is there to provide help when you need it."

Matos and Verkler found that men also live longer if they have a roommate. "It doesn't matter who the persn is, a parent, child orfreind," Verkler said. "We've found, however,that none of the alternatives are as conducive to a long life as a stable marriage. those are the man who live the longest, the men who are happily marrried."

Outstanding Teacher

Wilma DeCastro is an English teacher at Kennedy High Schol and, six months ago, was named the city's "Teacher ofthe Year." Today she resigned.

"All my life I wanted to be a teachher," DeCastro said. "Ive really enjoyed it, but I have two little girls and Can't afford it any longer. I want a good live for may family, and now wecan't afford to buy a decent house in a good neighborhood, a newcar, nice clothes, or so many of the other things we want. wee skimp on everything, even food."

Name _____   **Class** _____   **Date** _____

There years ago, DeCastro began to sell real estate during her sumer vacations. For th e last year, she has continued to sell real estate part-time, primarily weakends

"I can't do it any longer," she said. "I can't wrok two jobs, do a good job at both of the jobbs, and a.lso have time for my daughters, so I've decided to go into real estate full time. I can triple salary my salary. INN a few years, if I work hard, I should be able to do even better than that. eventually, I'd like togo into businss for myself."

Greg Hubbard, superintendent of the city's school system, said: "Of coures we're sorry to see her leave. We'd like to keep her, to be able to pay all our teachers mr more, espec ially our best teachers. But there's no moneey for higher salaries. NO one wants to pay higher taxes."

DeCastro is 28 and started teaching at the high schoo01 six years ago. she aws named "Teacher OF The Year" because of her popularity, but also because she inspired several studentsto start a literary maga zine that has won adozenprizes

EXERCISE 6: Format

INSTRUCTIONS: Edit the following news stories to conform to Associated Press style and to correct any errors of spelling, punctuation and grammar.

Heroic Girl

while walking to school this moningmorning, an 11-year-old girl noticed a gunman robbuing two clerkS in a convenence store on Colonial Drive

The girl, Kathryn Kunze of94 Jamestown Drive, raran to a nearby telepone, dialed 911, then returned to the store and noticed an empty car par ked naearby withits motor running. she reachedd inside, shut off the cars motor and took the keys.

"Imagine what the rober thought when he ran out of the storee, jumped into HIS car and realized the keys weregone," said Sgt. Tammy Dow. "she was one smart girl, and Brave, too."

Name _____   Class _____   Date _____

The Gunman went bavck into the stoer and asked the clerks there for the keys to there cars. Bothclerks, however, said that they had walked to work and did not own a car.

The gunman then walked to a near,by park, and the police Aarrested him there five minutse later.

William j. Chuey, 27, of 5710 michigan Ave was charrged with armed robbery.

Polic e officers later questioned the girl at school. "I saw this man with a gun, just like on telivision" she said. "Then I saw thecar. It was running, and I just figured it was the robbers, so I took his keys and ran here."

Kathryn's mother, said she was p'''proud -- and frightened -- by her daughters actions. "I'Mm proud she thought so quickly," Mrs. Lauren Kunze said. "But I don't wnat her to trfy anything like that ever again."

####

Roadbed Trails

RAilroads have abandoned hundreds of m iles of old roadbeds in the state, and the governortoday revealed plans to convert the roadbeds into trawils for bicyclists hikers, horseback riders and runners.

The govenor said her budget for nxextt year will include an extra $10 million for the Departmentof natural Resources, which will use the money to ac quire and maintainn the trials

"The initial outlay is modest," the gov. said. "But we hope the program will expand so, in five or 10 years,we'll have hundreds of miles of these trials. Eventually, the people using themshould be able to hike or ride from one end of the state to another."

A representative for the states railrods said that most will probably agree to sell their abandoned roadbeds tothe state, provided they receive a fair pricee,

Name _____ **Class** _____ **Date** _____

"We aren't us ing the roadbeds for anything," he said, "and there aren't many other buyers. they were our leasst profitable routes, and that's why we abandoned them."

During a press Conference this mohningthis morning, the governor added: "We need more land for recreation, and this is the prefect solution. wee think we can acquire the roadbeds for a reasonable price, annd we'll start with some of the mmost scenic. We'llalso concentrate, at least initialy, on roadbeds near the state's population centers, os they're conveni ent for a majority of the people using them."

THE governor said the

biggest expense, after acquiri;ng the roadbeds, will be improving their bridges.. "We'll need better flooring and railings to protect the public, and that will cost some money," she said. The railoads havve already tor n up the tracks,o selling them for scrap.

####

Repossessing Cars

Police Chief Barry Kopperud Wants to ebgin seizing t he cars driven by drunken drivers.

While testifyingbefore a legislative commmittee in the state capital this morning, Kopperud said police oficers in the state need the authority to to seize the vehicles used by motorists convicted three or more times of drunken driving. Kopperuds pproposal would al so apply to motorists convicted of driving with a license suspended or revoked because of drunken drving -- and to motorists convicted of driving undre the Influence of drugs.

"Were runninng across too many repeat offjenders," kopperud said. "They ignore the laws now in eff ect, and its time to do something about it. It doesn't do any good to just take away their lcenses. They'll drivewithout one."

Kopperud said some motorists in the statehave been convicted of drunken driving more than a dozentimes . "Weve gott peopel who've served a year in jail, some who've served five years," Kopperud said. "It doesn't seemtodo any good. weather they have a liense or not, they star"t to drink and drive again as soon as they get out. If wetake away their cars, they'll havetostop. U nless they're ultra-rich, there's a limit to howmany cars they can afford to buy."

####

Tobacco Ban

Beginning next fall, students in the citys public shcools will have to leave their cigarettes and other tobaco products at home.

The School Board last night voted 6 to 1 to BAN the possession and use of all obacco tobacco products on school grounds.

"The boards policy will apply to evferyone," said gary Hubbard, superin-tendent of schools. "its not just for ourstudents. The policy will also apply to our teachers, other school personnel and, in addition, to any visitors using our facilities."

Students found smoking on school property will be reprimanded for a firs t ofense, detained for a secnod and su;pended for three days for a third. School personnel will be reprimanded by their principal. Other people wlil be asked to stop using the tobacco products or to leave the school grounds.

"Previously," hubbard said, "we allowed stud ents to smokee inn some designated areas both inside and outside our bldgs.: in our football stadium s, for example. Its badfortheir health, and we decided last night that we weren't being consistent. It doesn't make any sense for us to tell students, in their classes, about the dangers of smoking, andthan to allow them to smokeunder our supervision. Besides, We were geting a lot of complaints from nonsmokesr."

Name _____   Class _____   Date _____

EXERCISES TO ACCOMPANY CHAPTER 4

The Language of News

EXERCISE 1: Recognizing and Correcting Newswriting Errors

SECTION I: AGREEMENT

INSTRUCTIONS: Edit the following sentences, correcting agreement and other errors.

1. The committee submits their data this weekend and expects it to help their church.

2. She said the company failed to earn enough to repay their loans, and she does not expect them to reopen.

3. The jury reached their verdict at 1 a.m., concluding that the media was guilty of libeling the restaurant and their twenty-two employees.

4. The decision allowed the city council to postpone their vote for a week, and they suggested that the sites developer design a plan to save more of it's trees.

5. A representative for the organization said they help anyone that is on welfare obtain some job training and raise their self esteem.

SECTION II: POSSESSIVES

INSTRUCTIONS: Edit the following sentences, correcting for possessives and other errors.

1. The womens car was parked nearby, and sheriffs deputies asked to see the owners drivers license.

2. The woman said she opposes assisted suicide "because a doctors job is to save peoples lives, not end them."

3. Last years outstanding teacher insisted that peoples complaints about the schools problems are mistaken.

4. Katrina Jones parents said there younger childrens teacher earned her bachelors degree in philosophy and her masters degree in eductaion.

5. Everyones money was stolen, and the neighborhood associations president warned that the police are no longer able to guarantee peoples safety in the citys poorest neighborhoods.

Name _____   Class _____   Date _____

SECTION III: PLACEMENT

INSTRUCTIONS: Rewrite these sentences, keeping related words and ideas together. Correct all errors.

1. The board of trustees voted 8–1 to fire the college president for his sexual misconduct during an emergency meeting Thursday morning.

2. On their arrival, the hotel manager took the guests' bags to their rooms.

3. The union representative urged Americans to support better working conditions for the nations migrant workers at the Unitarian church Sunday.

4. Jogging around campus, a thorn bush ripped a hole in Jill's shirt.

5. A suspect in the burglary case was arrested after a high-speed chase involving two lawn mowers stolen from a hardware store.

6. In the hope that the sun would come out, the softball game drew a large crowd.

SECTION IV: PERSONIFICATION

INSTRUCTIONS: Rewrite the following sentences, eliminating personification and other errors.

1. Slamming on its brakes, the car turned to the left, narrowly missing the dog.

2. The city said it cannot help the three businesses who asked for better lighting.

3. After detecting the outbreak, the hospital admitted that 7 babies born this month were infected, including one that died.

4. The Fire Department treated the child for smoke inhalation, then transported her to Mercy Hospital, which treated her broken legs.

5. The corporation, which denied any responsibility for the deaths, will appear in court next month.

SECTION V: PARALLEL FORM

INSTRUCTIONS: Rewrite these sentences in parallel form, and correct all errors.

1. He was charged with drunken driving and an expired drivers license.

2. Karen Kim was a full-time student, Air Force reservist, and she worked part-time for a veterinarian.

3. To join the club, one must be a sophomore, junior or senior; studying journalism; be in good academic standing; and have demonstrated professional journalistic ability.

Name _____   Class _____   Date _____

4. The mayor warned that the neighborhoods high crime rate causes residents to flee, contributes to more unemployment for workers, and the city loses tax revenue, along with lowering everyones property values.

5. She said the other advantages of owning her own business include being independent, not having a boss, flexible hours and less stress.

SECTION VI: MULTIPLE ERRORS

INSTRUCTIONS: Rewrite the following sentences, correcting all errors. Some sentences contain more than one error.

1. A sheriffs deputy saw the teenagers Chevrolet pull out of the alley, driving recklessly without its headlines on, and arrested it's driver.

2. The city also said that they cannot silence Sandra Elliston, the woman that fears pollution is likely to effect the neighborhoods 300 residents.

3. Seeking more money, publicity, and to help the poor, the churchs members said it wants the city to help it by providing food and offer housing for the homeless.

4. The Public Works Department said they could pave the developments road themselves for less than $1.2 million, the Roess Company submitted a bid of $2.74 million.

5. A jury awarded almost $10.5 million to the operators of an abortion clinic that charged that picketers tormented them and there clients. The clinics operators praised the jury's verdict, saying their courage and understanding set a needed precedent.

EXERCISE 2: Vocabulary

INSTRUCTIONS: Words with different meanings often look or sound similar. As a journalist, you should be familiar with these words and use them correctly. Cross out the wrong words in the following sentences, leaving only the correct ones. Consult The Associated Press Stylebook for preferred usage. Also correct errors in style and possessives. If you need help, the rules for forming possessives appear in Appendix C, and AP style rules are summarized in Appendix B.

1. The (cite/sight/site) chosen by the City for (it's/its) new office building could (affect/effect) parking in that part of town.

2. The United States army general was able to (envelop/envelope) the enemy in (fewer/less) than 24 hours, capturing (more than/over) 7,000 soldiers (who/whom/which) were (than/then) disarmed.

3. The fire (marshall/marshal) said it will cost (about/around) 100,000 dollars to repair the apartment complex, where a dozen (people/persons) lived before Friday's fire (burnt/burned) most of the building.

Name _____ **Class** _____ **Date** _____

4. The elementary school (principal/principle) said Mister Smith is a man of high (principal/principle) and deserves the (reward/award) as teacher of the year.

5. The (blond/blonde) girl (complimented/complemented) her friend on the new shoes (that/which) she bought on sale for just ten dollars.

6. The Governor's (aid/aide) said the rally on the steps of the state (Capital/Capitol) drew 10 thousand people despite the bad (weather/whether).

7. The mayor said city employee's (moral/morale) is very low and blamed it on (they're/their/there) recent pay cut, (that/which) was (adapted/adopted) by City (council/counsel) last month.

8. John and his (fiance/fiancee), (who/whom) he met at college, checked the (calendar/calender) and said (their/there/they're) sure they want to have the party on May 1st.

9. That (desert/dessert) was a tasty (complement/compliment) to our meals'.

10. He (adviced/advised) the investors to (altar/alter) their plans (because/since) it would be difficult to (ensure/insure) everyone's cooperation.

11. Rather (than/then) (censor/censure) the 9 bank (trustees/trusties), he wants a new state (ordinance/ordnance) to govern (their/there/they're) behavior.

12. The woman (who/whom/that) came to my (aide/aid) when I fell on the sidewalk is a (alumna/alumnae/alumni/alumnus) of Princeton.

13. The antique carriage began to (role/roll) (foreword/forward) until a (loose/lose) wheel fell off, making it impossible to travel any (farther/further).

14. The (forth/fourth) group of veterans entered the (alley/ally), which veers south at a forty-five degree (angel/angle), (then/than) marched 7 more (blocs/blocks).

15. Mother helped to (canvas/canvass) the neighborhood today with (fliers/flyers) for dad's new store, and she said she needs to (lay/lie) down for a while before making dinner.

16. The book (entitled/titled) *Betrayal* estimates that the (trail/trial) will last (fewer/less) than 10 days and (implies/infers) that the jury will find the defendent (innocent/not guilty).

17. They (hanged/hung) the controversial painting in a school hallway and want to know (who's/whose) side (your/you're) likely to favor.

18. The minister (prayed/preyed) for the swift recovery of the 8 (persons/people) (who/whom) (received/suffered/sustained) injuries during last night's storm.

19. The children said (their/there/they're) families (emigrated/immigrated) from Asia and are (liable/libel/likely) to move (farther/further) South.

Name _____ Class _____ Date _____

20. The large (bloc/block) of voters opposed to the plan (convinced/persuaded) Board members to reread the (data/datum) and (altar/alter) the five (criteria/criterion) for (choosing/chosing) the school's architect.

EXERCISE 3: Vocabulary

INSTRUCTIONS: Words with different meanings often look or sound familiar. As a journalist, you should be familiar with these words and use them correctly. Cross out the wrong words in the following sentences, leaving only the correct ones. Consult The Associated Press Stylebook for preferred usage. Also, correct errors in style and possessives. If you need help, the rules for forming possessives appear in Appendix C, and AP style rules are summarized in Appendix B.

1. A (pole/poll) conducted by the candidates supporters showed 60 (per cent/percent) of the (persons/people) surveyed planned to vote for (he/him) in the Nov. election.

2. Her (fiance/fiancee) (implied/inferred) that her softball teams (moral/morale) was (effected/affected) when the coach was replaced.

3. The jogger became (conscience/conscious) of several cars behind her and then decided to (alter/altar) her course, even though the new route took her up (to/too) many (ascents/assents).

4. I am (confidant/confident) that you will win the leading (role/roll) in this years play, but Bill thinks (your/you're) likely to (lose/loose) it to Beth.

5. Nancys Mother will (lay/lie) out a blanket for her in case she wants to (lay/lie) down before Robert comes over to visit.

6. The woman, an (emigrant/immigrant) (born/borne) in Irelands (capital/capitol) of Dublin, said she wants to (aid/aide) the nine-member city (consul/council/counsel).

7. The company's new president is an (alumna/alumnae/alumni/alumnus) of the local university (who/whom) started her speech with an amusing (anecdote/antidote) to put the (personal/personnel) at ease about her hiring.

8. The teachers said they will need (more than/over) 100 volunteers to help with all the student's programs on this year's (calendar/calender), but the (principal/principle) warned that (fewer/less) than a dozen parents were likely (to/too) offer their assistance.

9. To (ensure/insure) (its/it's) success, the editors updated the (media's/medium's) content, thereby increasing its circulation and prestige.

10. In his report, the police officer said the (burglar/robber/swindler/thief) who broke into the home at 313 North Twenty-first St (ravaged/ravished) only a closet, and added that the crime was the most (bazaar/bizarre) he has seen in his 6-yr. career.

Name _____ Class _____ Date _____

11. George just joined the country club, but he already is (adapt/adept/adopt) at (convincing/persuading) the (trustees/trusties) to (waive/wave) the restrictions on guests using the facilitys.

12. The judges (complemented/complimented) all the teams but said the girls in the (forth/fourth) lane swam (farther/further) than any of their competitiors.

13. Barbara said the (foul/fowl) odor coming from the next room was (liable/libel/likely) to make other (people/persons) sick regardless of (weather/whether) they entered the room.

14. (More than/Over) fifty (persons/people) (comprised/composed) the team of volunteers (who's/whose) job it was to address and seal the (envelops/envelopes).

15. The reporter's story about the bicycle (trail/trial) quoted several people who said (its/it's) (to/too) dangerous (since/because) they (received/suffered/sustained) injuries as they tried to (pedal/peddle) (farther/further) North.

16. Carla (dyed/died) her hair (blond/blonde) because she heard that (blonds/blondes) have more fun.

17. The (statue/statute) of a misshapen (angel/angle) on the church (altar/alter) caused a (miner/minor) controversy among the two-hundred member congregation.

18. Acting on the (advise/advice) of (they're/there/their) older sister, the twins bought prom dresses that (complemented/complimented) each other.

19. The (legislators/legislatures) vowed to fight the Governor's budget, saying they have the (block/bloc) of votes needed to veto the spending plan.

20. (There/They're/Their) the ones who are trying to raise 1,000 dollars for a new (plaque/plague) on the (sight/site/cite) of the famous Civil War Battle, (that/which) occurred (about/around) 2 miles from the center of town.

EXERCISE 4: Verbs

SECTION I: AVOIDING USE OF NOUNS AS VERBS

INSTRUCTIONS: Rewrite the following sentences, eliminating the use of nouns as verbs.

1. She authored a new book on the Vietnam War.

2. The soldiers were headquartered in Kuwait City.

3. The class interfaced with the teacher by email.

4. They inked a new contract with the record company.

5. They were shotgunned to death, and their bodies will be autopsied Friday.

Name _____   Class _____   Date _____

SECTION II: USING STRONGER VERBS

INSTRUCTIONS: List three stronger, more active and descriptive verbs that could replace the verbs in the following sentences.

1. The soccer goalie was able to prevent the last shot.

2. That art history book has many photographs.

3. She got a new car.

4. The politician did a survey of local voters.

5. More than 300 people are employed at the plant.

SECTION III: USING STRONGER VERBS

INSTRUCTIONS: Rewrite the following sentences, using stronger verbs. Also use normal word order (subject, verb, direct object).

1. The car is in need of a new paint job.

2. He was planning to open a restaurant in Houston.

3. The professor was able to interest many students in his classes.

4. The preschool nutrition program is set up so that the cost is paid by the state.

5. A short circuit in the electrical wiring at the church was the cause of the fire.

6. The cost of a ticket for admission to the amusement park is $25.

7. A trip to the beach is what Karen and David are planning for this summer.

8. To obtain extra money to pay for college, John has picked up a second job.

9. It was suggested by the moderator that the panel participants may want to take a break.

10. The reservations she made at the hotel were for three rooms.

EXERCISE 5: Avoiding Common Errors

SECTION I: AVOIDING GRAMMATICAL AND VOCABULARY ERRORS

INSTRUCTIONS: Rewrite the following sentences, correcting their wording.

1. The city council voted on the motion they made to accept the bids.

2. Police officers arrested the man that had broken into the store.

Name _____ Class _____ Date _____

3. Saying the administration would support her, the professor said they wanted her to take the position.

4. The men and women that are members of the committee hope to settle the dispute soon.

5. The hospital board plans to attend the opening of the new wing of the hospital they approved last year.

SECTION II: KEEPING RELATED WORDS AND IDEAS TOGETHER

INSTRUCTIONS: Rewrite these sentences, improving the word placement.

1. The construction workers saved the drowning boys who were working at the site.

2. The girl was taken to a hospital for observation by her parents.

3. The award was presented to the class which represents perfect attendance.

4. Robert Allen Wiese was sentenced to one year in prison after pleading guilty to violating probation by Circuit Court judge Samuel McGregor.

5. A suspect in the burglary case was arrested after a high-speed chase involving two lawnmowers stolen from a hardware store.

SECTION III: AVOIDING IMPRECISION

INSTRUCTIONS: Rewrite the following sentences, making them as precise as possible.

1. The woman bought the dress she saw in the window walking down the street.

2. The man was killed instantly after he was struck by the train.

3. After paying a $325 fine, the dog was free to go home with its owner.

4. The judge sentenced the corporate executive to 10 years in prison after pleading guilty to five counts of fraud.

5. Minutes after the man left the bar, he collided with a car that totally destroyed his pickup truck.

SECTION IV: DEFINING AND EXPLAINING

INSTRUCTIONS: Define or explain each of the large numbers or unfamiliar terms in the following sentences.

1. Their son has meningitis.

2. A single B-2 Stealth bomber costs $800 million.

3. Pioneer 10, a satellite launched on March 2, 1972, is 4.2 billion miles from the sun.

Name _____   Class _____   Date _____

SECTION V: AVOIDING CLICHÉS

INSTRUCTIONS: Rewrite the following sentences, eliminating clichés.

1. He said the cold soda really hit the spot on a hot day.

2. Police are trying to find the serial rapist and halt his reign of terror.

3. The mayor had won a reputation for trying to sweep problems under the rug.

4. The bicycle race got off to a good start with a see-saw battle between the two leaders.

5. The governor said he make a last-ditch stand to save the legislation he was proposing to the state senate.

SECTION VI: AVOIDING UNNECESSARY PARENTHESES

INSTRUCTIONS: Eliminate the parentheses and other errors from the following sentences.

1. She (the mayor) said (in response to a question about property taxes) that she opposes any such proposal (to increase them).

2. Despite the loss (now estimated at $4.2 million), he said the company should be able to pay all their debts before the deadline (Dec. 30).

3. The governor predicted, "They (members of the Legislature) will approve the proposal (to increase the sales tax) within 60 days."

SECTION VII: AVOIDING THE NEGATIVE

INSTRUCTIONS: Rewrite the following sentences in positive form.

1. Not until last year were they able to buy their new home.

2. The test was not that easy to finish in the allotted time.

3. The students do not have any limitations on which songs they can choose.

4. The car was parked not far away.

5. The mayor said she would not be disinclined to vote against the motion.

SECTION VIII: IMPROVING SENTENCES

INSTRUCTIONS: Rewrite the following sentences, correcting all their errors.

1. He and she was planning to go to the concert.

2. The fire occurred Sunday night in a basement room used by the school band, causing an estimated $30,000 damage and destroyed 80 of their uniforms.

3. The physician, an alumni of the university, came under fire for his comments about the schools medical program.

4. The tragic accident was finally cleaned up by police and firefighters so traffic lanes could reopen.

5. She wants to establish a program where convicted juveniles would be required to perform some sort of community service and not go to jail.

EXERCISE 6: Spelling

INSTRUCTIONS: Cross off the word that is misspelled in each of the following pairs. Always use the spelling recommended by The Associated Press.

1. a lot/alot
2. acceptable/acceptible
3. accidently/accidentally
4. accommodate/accomodate
5. advertising/advertizing
6. adviser/advisor
7. afterward/afterwards
8. alright/all right
9. baptize/baptise
10. boy friend/boyfriend
11. broccoli/brocolli
12. canceled/cancelled
13. catagorized/categorized
14. cemetery/cemetary
15. comming/coming
16. commited/committed
17. congradulations/congratulations
18. conscious/concious

19. contraversial/controversial
20. credability/credibility
21. critized/criticized
22. cryed/cried
23. defendant/defendent
24. desert/dessert (food)
25. despite/dispite
26. deterrant/deterrent
27. dilema/dilemma
28. disastrous/disasterous
29. dispise/despise
30. elite/elete
31. embarass/embarrass
32. emphasize/emphacize
33. employe/employee
34. endorsed/indorsed
35. exhorbitant/exorbitant
36. existance/existence

Name _____   Class _____   Date _____

37. explaination/explanation

38. fascination/facination

39. favortism/favoritism

40. Febuary/February

41. fourty/forty

42. fulfil/fulfill

43. glamour/glamor

44. goverment/government

45. guerrilla/guerilla

46. harassment/harrassment

47. humorous/humerous

48. independant/independent

49. indispensable/indispensible

50. infered/inferred

51. innuendo/inuendo

52. irrate/irate

53. irregardless/regardless

54. it's/its (possessive)

55. janiter/janitor

56. judgement/judgment

57. kindergarten/kindergarden

58. license/liscense

59. lightning/lightening

60. likelyhood/likelihood

61. magazines/magasines

62. municipal/municiple

63. nickles/nickels

64. noticeable/noticable

65. occasionally/ocassionally

66. occured/occurred

67. oppertunity/opportunity

68. per cent/percent

69. permissable/permissible

70. personel/personnel

71. persue/pursue

72. picknicking/picnicking

73. plagiarism/plagarism

74. practice/practise

75. priviledge/privilege

76. protester/protestor

77. questionnaire/questionaire

78. receive/recieve

79. reckless/wreckless

80. re-elect/reelect

81. refering/referring

82. gardless/regardless

83. resturant/restaurant

84. roomate/roommate

85. saleries/salaries

86. sandwich/sandwhich

Name _____   Class _____   Date _____

87. seige/siege

88. separate/seperate

89. sergeant/sargeant

90. sizable/sizeable

91. sophmore/sophomore

92. souvenir/sovenir

93. stab/stabb

94. strickly/strictly

95. suing/sueing

96. summarize/summerize

97. surgery/surgury

98. surprise/surprize

99. taxi/taxy

100. teen-ager/teenager

101. temperature/temperture

102. tendancy/tendency

103. their/thier

104. totaled/totalled

105. toward/towards

106. transfered/transferred

107. tries/trys

108. truely/truly

109. until/untill

110. useable/usable

111. vacinate/vaccinate

112. vacuum/vaccum

113. valedictorian/valdictorian

114. vetoes/vetos

115. victum/victim

116. villain/villan

117. Wednesday/Wedesday

118. wierd/weird

119. writing/writting

120. yield/yield

EXERCISE 7: Spelling

INSTRUCTIONS: Cross off the word that is misspelled in each of the following pairs. Always use the spelling recommended by The Associated Press.

1. abberation/aberration

2. abbreviate/abreviate

3. abdomen/abdoman

4. absence/absense

5. accessible/accessable

6. acknowlegement/acknowledgment

7. acquaintance/acquantance

8. acter/actor

9. adherant/adherent

10. admissable/admissible

Name _____   Class _____   Date _____

11. admited/admitted

12. affidavit/afidavit

13. allready/already

14. alotted/alloted

15. alphabet/alphebet

16. ambulance/ambulence

17. ammendment/amendment

18. among/amoung

19. apologize/apologise

20. apparantly/apparently

21. arguement/argument

22. arithematic/arithmetic

23. assassinate/assasinate

24. athlete/athlite

25. auxiliary/auxillary

26. ax/axe

27. baby sit/baby-sit

28. bachelor's/bachelors degree

29. backward/backwards

30. baloney/balogna

31. barbecue/barbeque

32. basically/basicly

33. becoming/becomming

34. believable/beleivable

35. beneficial/benificial

36. broadcast/broadcasted

37. bureacracy/bureaucracy

38. burglars/burglers

39. Caribbean/Carribean

40. catagorized/categorized

41. catalog/catalogue

42. catastrophe/catastraphe

43. champagne/champayne

44. changeable/changable

45. chauffeur/chaufeur

46. cigarettes/cigaretes

47. commited/committed

48. comparable/comperable

49. concensus/consensus

50. contemptible/contemptable

51. definately/definitely

52. demagogue/demogog

53. dependent/dependant

54. desireable/desirable

55. destroyed/distroyed

56. deterant/deterrent

57. develop/develope

58. deviding/dividing

59. disasterous/disastrous

60. discrimination/descrimination

Name _____   Class _____   Date _____

61. drunkenness/drunkeness

62. exaggerate/exagerate

63. existence/existance

64. expelled/expeled

65. familiar/familar

66. fiery/fierey

67. forward/forwards

68. fourty/forty

69. goodby/goodbye

70. grammar/grammer

71. guarante/guarantee

72. hazzard/hazard

73. hemorrhage/hemorrage

74. heros/heroes

75. hitchiker/hitchhiker

76. imminent/imminant

77. imposter/impostor

78. innuendo/inuendo

79. involveing/involving

80. labelled/labeled

81. layed/laid

82. liaison/liason

83. likeable/likable

84. limousine/limousene

85. loneliness/lonelyness

86. maintnance/maintenance

87. mathematics/mathmatics

88. medias/media (plural)

89. millionaire/millionnaire

90. missile/missle

91. misspell/mispell

92. mortgage/morgage

93. mosquitos/mosquitoes

94. necesary/necessary

95. omitted/ommited

96. paniced/panicked

97. payed/paid

98. persistent/persistant

99. perspiration/persperation

100. potatoes/potatos

101. practise/practice

102. precede/preceed

103. preparing/prepairing

104. prevalent/prevalant

105. professor/proffessor

106. prominent/prominant

107. pryed/pried

108. realised/realized

109. receive/recieve

110. repetition/repitition

Name _____ **Class** _____ **Date** _____

111. resturant/restaurant

112. saboteur/sabateur

113. sheriff/sherrif

114. singular/singuler

115. sophmore/sophomore

116. survivors/survivers

117. tenative/tentative

118. traveled/travelled

119. wintry/wintery

120. worrys/worries

Name _____   Class _____   Date _____

EXERCISES TO ACCOMPANY CHAPTER 5

Libel, Privacy and Newsgathering Issues

EXERCISE 1: Libel

INSTRUCTIONS: Write an essay analyzing whether the news organization in the following situation can be sued successfully for libel. Consider all the elements of a libel case and how likely the plaintiff would be to prove each. Consider also whether the plaintiff is a public official, public figure or private individual. Finally, consider what defenses the news organization might use.

When Local 1313 of the Municipal Employees Union and the Beacon City Council negotiated a new labor contract for the city's employees last year, the union was represented by Sam Fong, its chief negotiator. The Beacon negotiations were stressful and stormy, with accusations of bad-faith bargaining made by both sides. At one point, the union threatened to strike if its demands were not met.

As the strike deadline approached, Hilda Jackson, reporter for the Beacon Daily Light, prepared a story that profiled Fong and described the union's negotiating strategy. Jackson talked to a number of people familiar with Fong and the way he conducted labor negotiations.

Jackson's story included the comments of Paula Williams, a city councilwoman, who said during a council meeting: "Fong is a first-rate bastard. That S.O.B. is trying to extort a fortune from the city. If we give him what he wants, we'll be broke, and if we don't, he'll shut down the city with a strike."

Another of Jackson's sources is Ben Davis, a union member with a grudge against Fong and a history of alcoholism. Davis said Fong had promised to keep union members informed about negotiations and to get their advice and guidance, but instead he had kept the members in the dark. Davis also said he suspected that union money had been used to hire prostitutes for union officials. He said a union bookkeeper had information that could confirm his story, but Jackson did not talk to him. Nevertheless, she included Davis's allegations in her story.

Jackson also reported that Fong had been convicted of automobile theft when he was 19 and had spent five years in a state penitentiary. Because Jackson failed to read the entire record of the case, her report was incorrect. Fong had served only 18 months of his five-year sentence and was placed on parole because of his good behavior.

Immediately after Jackson's story was published, Fong's wife sued him for divorce, alleging adultery and citing the allegation that union officials had engaged prostitutes as an instance of adultery. National union leaders also commenced an investigation of how Fong was spending his expense account money. The national union concluded that the charges of misuse of union money were groundless, but it dismissed Fong anyway for having failed to disclose his conviction for auto theft when he applied for his job.

Fong sued the Beacon Daily Light for libel.

Name _____   Class _____   Date _____

EXERCISE 2: **Libel**

INSTRUCTIONS: Write an essay analyzing whether the news organization in this situation can be sued successfully for libel. Consider all the elements of a libel case and how likely the plaintiffs would be to prove each. Consider also whether each plaintiff is a public official, public figure or private individual. Finally, consider what defenses the news organization might use.

U.S. policy toward the Central American country of Costa Grande, where there is a civil war, has been the subject of extensive debate in Congress, a key issue in some congressional elections and a major news story for some months. As part of its coverage of the topic, the Continental Broadcasting Co.'s Nightly News program has investigated and broadcast a story alleging that three people, including a prominent federal official, were involved in sending arms and supplies to rebels in Costa Grande in violation of U.S. law.

One was Russell Starr, a retired Army general, who is considered an expert on Central American insurgency movements. He is president of an organization that has promoted the cause of the Costa Grande rebels. He has written newspaper and magazine pieces about the justness of the rebels' cause and has defended them on television talk shows. The second figure is Ronda Vernon, who recently became the third wealthiest person in the country when she inherited the fortune her father earned in the computer software business. Vernon rarely appears in public and never comments on political matters, but through various trust funds that she and her family control, she has donated millions of dollars to controversial groups, including the Costa Grande rebels. The last key figure in the Nightly News piece is Sean Grady, assistant secretary of state for Central American affairs, the member of the administration with primary responsibility for formulating and carrying out U.S. policy in that region.

The Nightly News story said that Starr had used dummy corporations and numbered Swiss bank accounts to channel money from his organization to the purchase of arms and supplies for the rebels. Several men involved in the illegal arms trade, all convicted felons, told reporters about Starr's financial arrangements. The information from the arms dealers was corroborated for the most part with information from several reliable staff members of congressional committees. The congressional staffers were familiar with classified information on Starr's dealings. Starr denied any wrongdoing and steered reporters to sources who would back him up. But the Nightly News reporters ignored Starr's sources because none had any inside knowledge.

The Nightly News said that Vernon had contributed $3 million to Starr's organization in full knowledge that some of the money was being sent illegally to the Costa Grande rebels. This part of the story was based on interviews with various people who had helped manage some of the Vernon family trust funds and on financial statements. Because of a reporter's arithmetic error, however, the Nightly News exaggerated the size of Vernon's contributions to the Costa Grande rebels by $700,000.

As for Grady, the news broadcast said he had used his official position in order to persuade the FBI to ignore the trio's illegal activities. Nightly News' only source for this was another State Department official, who is known to covet Grady's job. The official said he learned about Grady's efforts to obstruct any federal investigation of Starr and Vernon when a glitch in the telephone system enabled him to overhear a conversation between Grady and an FBI agent. The network's reporters failed to check with the bureau to find out whether any of its agents had even tried to investigate the flow of arms and cash to the Costa Grande rebels.

Starr, Vernon, and Grady all sued the network for libel.

Name _____   Class _____   Date _____

EXERCISE 3: Privacy

INSTRUCTIONS: Write an essay analyzing whether the news organization in this situation can be sued successfully for invasion of privacy. Consider all four forms of invasion of privacy and decide whether the plaintiff would be able to prove any of them.

Jasmine Lynd is a model-turned-actress who has appeared on the covers of many fashion magazines and in several major motion pictures. She attended a reception at the governor's mansion and stayed late for a private cocktail with the governor. The next day, Lynd reported to the police that the governor had raped her. The incident drew intense coverage from the press, including the Weekly Intelligencer, a tabloid newspaper sold mainly in supermarkets. In the past, Lynd had angered Intelligencer editors by refusing requests for interviews and threatening libel suits. One editor told the reporters covering the case, "This is our chance to pay her back."

Lynd would not talk to Intelligencer reporters, so they spoke to a number of her friends and acquaintances. One friend described Lynd's high school career, saying that she had been a "party girl" who had barely passed her courses and had frequently been in trouble with school authorities. Another source mentioned that Lynd had overcome, with great effort, a severe stuttering problem as a teenager.

Other Intelligencer reporters examined court records and learned that Lynd had three arrests for speeding and one for drunken driving. Other records showed that her husband had divorced her because she had been unfaithful. Her ex-husband said in an interview with reporters that he had discovered Lynd's infidelity when she gave him a venereal disease she had picked up from her lover, a professional wrestler. The wrestler told reporters that Lynd had an irrational fear of food preservatives, chewed her fingernails compulsively and always slept in the nude. Lynd has denied none of these statements.

The divorce records on file in district court also provided reporters with information about Lynd's finances, including the fact that she had purchased a controlling interest in a television production business and several pieces of commercial real estate, all of which more than tripled in value in only two years. One of Lynd's former friends, a woman who had known her in high school but had not seen her for 15 years, said that Lynd never made a business investment without consulting the famous astrologer Wesley Wilson. Wilson denied that Lynd was one of his clients, but the Intelligencer published the assertion anyway.

The Intelligencer's editors dispatched two teams of photographers to get photos for the story. One team followed Lynd wherever she went—work, shopping, social events—constantly snapping photos. On one occasion, trying to get a photo of her driving on the freeway, they maneuvered their car so close to hers that she swerved to avoid them and grazed a safety railing. Another team of photographers stationed themselves at the side of a highway on a hill overlooking Lynd's expensive home. From that location, the photographers used powerful telephoto lenses to get pictures of Lynd sunbathing and swimming in her back yard (which is surrounded by a high privacy fence).

Even though Lynd had not talked to reporters since she charged the governor with rape, the Intelligencer promoted its story about her with an advertisement in several newspapers saying, "Meet Jasmine Lynd. Find out what Lynd told the Intelligencer that she would tell no one else. You can depend on the Intelligencer—just as Lynd does—to deliver the truth!"

Lynd has filed a lawsuit alleging that the Weekly Intelligencer has invaded her privacy by placing her in a false light, giving publicity to private facts, intruding upon her solitude and seclusion and appropriating her name and likeness.

Name _____   Class _____   Date _____

EXERCISE TO ACCOMPANY CHAPTER **6**

Ethics

EXERCISE 1: Stories That Raise Ethical Concerns

INSTRUCTIONS: Write a news story using the facts below. Identify and deal with the various ethical issues each story presents. Write a separate essay explaining why you dealt with the ethical issues as you did.

BOY'S MURDER

Yesterday George Claunch, a 15-year-old high school student in your city, was stabbed to death. A student at Kennedy High School, he was found inside a vacant house at 482 Fern Creek Dr. His body was found by police answering an anonymous call to them and was found tied to a chair with his hands tied behind his back and stabbed multiple times in the chest. There was evidence of torture preceding death: of cigarette burns and bruises as he had apparently been beaten. Police continue to search for answers in the case. The victim's older brother, Tony, 19, today complained, "The cops aren't doing enough about his case. 'Cause of who he was they don't care." Tony acknowledges that his brother, the youngest of five siblings, had his fair share of run-ins with the law, that he was in and out of juvenile detention centers, cut classes, used marijuana, and may have belonged to a gang, although that is not known for sure at this point in time. For stealing a car he was on probation. The family is now dealing with its grief and searching for answers. A local police officer investigating the case, Detective Allison Biaggi, said the victim was apparently, they suspect, dealing drugs when he was killed, but police have not determined an exact motive, although there were drugs found at the scene. Those who might have information on the victim's death, friends, acquaintances, even relatives, refuse to cooperate with detectives, Biaggi said. Another brother, Raymond, said, "I haven't accepted it yet. I fault myself a little for what happened. I think he wanted love and didn't get it. Our father died four years ago, and that confused him in a way. My mother really loved him, but he wanted to do his own thing even when she told him not to. He never listened. He'd do his own thing, and that's what always got him into trouble, plus the guys he ran with weren't good people. It was them that got him in trouble." George Claunch was the son of Amy Claunch of 2481 Seasons Court, Apt. B.

Name _____   Class _____   Date _____

EXERCISES TO ACCOMPANY CHAPTER **7**

Basic News Leads

EXERCISE 1: Evaluating Good and Bad Leads

INSTRUCTIONS: Critically evaluate the following leads. Select the best leads and explain why they are effective. In addition, point out the flaws in the remaining leads. As you evaluate the leads, look for lessons—"do's and don'ts"—that you can apply to your own work.

1. A Baptist minister was convicted of drunken driving Tuesday and sentenced to 30 days in jail after a jury saw a police video of his failed sobriety test.

2. During a press conference in her office at 8 a.m. today, Mayor Sabrina Datolli spoke about the city's need for more parks.

3. With no debate, the City Council passed an ordinance Thursday to help fight crime by installing more street lights in three neighborhoods.

4. Loans become a popular way for students to conquer costs of college.

5. The campus is home to a variety of stray and wild animals.

6. Four years ago AIDS victim Edwin Jimenez, 22, learned he had only six months to live.

7. Do not cross off December 1 in your countdown toward Christmas. Instead, make plans to attend World AIDS Day on the Campus Green.

8. A panel of seven local journalism professionals discussed important media issues, including the role of the press, at the university Tuesday.

9. The week of Homecoming will be filled with numerous activities and freebies for students.

10. The right to bear arms may soon be taken away from anyone who steps onto public school grounds in the city.

11. A teen-age driver lost control of her car Tuesday night, paralyzing herself and killing a passenger. A 16-year-old riding in the back seat walked away only scratched and bruised.

12. Around 3 p.m. Friday a bank on Hillcrest Avenue was the scene of a daring daylight robbery and shooting.

13. Courses taught online offer an alternative to the traditional college classroom learning experience.

14. One year ago an accrediting agency criticized the college for using too many adjuncts (part-time faculty members). Since then, the college has reduced its number of adjuncts from 769 to 749.

15. Fred's restaurant at 1550 W. Colonial Drive was the location of a burglary Monday afternoon.

16. A 15-year-old boy slipped off the trunk of a moving car. His head hit asphalt and left a stain of blood on the spot. The boy was dead.

17. Spray-painted pitch forks and crowns are appearing on walls throughout the city. The symbols are trademarks of the Crips, a Los Angeles-based gang with members across the nation.

EXERCISE 2: Writing Leads

SECTION I: CONDENSING LENGTHY LEADS

INSTRUCTIONS: Condense each of these leads to no more than two typed lines, or about 20 words.

1. Maggie Baile, 28, of 810 N. Ontario Ave., an employee at the Halstini Manufacturing Plant, 810 Hall Road, suffered second- and third-degree burns at 2:15 p.m. yesterday when sparks from her welder's torch started a fire that quickly spread through the factory, causing nearly $1 million in damage and totally destroying the facility.

2. During a regularly scheduled meeting that began in its chambers at 8 p.m. last night, the City Council voted 5 to 2, after nearly 3 hours of debate, in favor of a proposal which, for the convenience of pedestrians, will require developers to construct a sidewalk in front of every new home and subdivision in the city.

SECTION II: USING THE PROPER SENTENCE STRUCTURE

INSTRUCTIONS: Rewrite the following leads, using the normal word order: subject, verb, direct object. Avoid starting the leads with a long clause or phrase. You may want to divide some of the leads into several sentences or paragraphs.

1. Saying that he had concluded that no benefit would come to anyone from the imprisonment of a 51-year-old woman who killed two teenagers while driving while intoxicated last summer, Circuit Court Judge Bruce R. Levine today suspended the woman's driver's license for five years and sentenced her to one year in the county jail, then suspended her jail sentence on the conditions that she seek professional help for her chronic alcoholism and pay all the teenagers' medical and funeral expenses.

2. Because the victim contributed in large measure to his own death by refusing medical attention that might have saved his life after the incident, James K. Arico, the 47-year-old man accused of stabbing him in the chest during an argument seven months ago, was allowed to plead guilty to assault today and was sentenced to six months in the county jail. He had been charged with murder.

Name _____ Class _____ Date _____

SECTION III: EMPHASIZING THE NEWS

INSTRUCTIONS: Rewrite the following leads, emphasizing the news, not the attribution. Limit the attributions to a few words and place them at the end, not the beginning, of the leads.

1. During a meeting in her office in Washington, D.C., today, the secretary of Health and Human Services told a group of health care specialists that American men and women who practice "wellness," a program of health promotion and disease prevention, can expect to live 11 years longer than people who neglect their health.

2. Tracy Tibitts, Lisa Drolshagen and Dorothy Brayton, all members of the Delta Delta Delta sorority at Iowa State University, appeared in a local courtroom this morning and testified that the defendant, Steven House, appeared drunk when he got into his car to leave the party moments before he struck and killed the pedestrian.

SECTION IV: COMBINING MULTISENTENCE LEADS

INSTRUCTIONS: Rewrite each of the following leads in a single sentence.

1. Acting on a tip, four detectives staked out a restaurant at 12:50 a.m. this morning and foiled an armed robbery. While posing as customers and employees, they observed two men with guns approach a cashier. The detectives captured both men.

2. Two city officials resigned today. Both had been criticized for abusing their positions. Mechanics at the city garage complained that both officials had them repair and wash and wax their cars. One of the city officials was the mayor. The other was her assistant. They never paid for any of the services.

SECTION V: STRESSING THE UNUSUAL

INSTRUCTIONS: Write only the lead for each of the following stories.

1. Daniel J. Silverbach is a policeman in your community. Last year, because of his heroic rescue of seven persons held at gunpoint during a robbery, Police Chief Barry Kopperud named him the departments Police Officer of the Year. Kopperud fired Silverbach when he reported for duty at 7 a.m. today. The department adopted certain grooming standards, and Kopperud said Silverbachs mustache was a quarter inch too long and his sideburns a half inch too long, and he refused to trim them. Kopperud added that he warned Silverbach a month ago to trim his hair, then ordered him to do so at the first of last week. He fired him for failing to obey the order of a superior officer.

2. Terri Snow of 3418 Hazel St. is a nurse at Mercy Hospital. She is married to Dale Snow, a former eighth-grade science teacher at Mays Junior High School. Snow was crippled after a diving accident three years ago, when his arms and legs were paralyzed. He met his wife at the hospital, where he was a patient, and they were married last month. Now state officials have suggested that they get a divorce. Before his marriage, Snow received $345 a month from the state's Department of Social Services and a monthly $792 federal Supplemental Security Income payment. Because of his wife's income, he is no

longer eligible for the payments, and the couple says without the payments they cannot afford to pay for Snow's continuing medical treatments and special diet. State officials have advised them that Snow will again become eligible for the aid if they get a divorce. The officials refused to talk to reporters, however.

3. Cremation is rising in popularity. Nearly 30 percent of the people who die in your state are now cremated. The Funeral Directors Association in your state met at noon yesterday and discussed a growing problem. The ashes of nearly 50 percent of those people they cremate are never claimed by family members, friends or anyone else, so they are stored in the funeral homes, and the directors want to dispose of them but are uncertain of their legal right to do so. They voted to ask the state legislature to pass a bill that spells out disposal procedures. The bill they propose would require funeral homes to make every effort to settle, with the family of the deceased, the desired disposal method. Families would have up to 90 days to pick up the remains or to specify what they want done with them. After 90 days, the funeral homes would be free to get rid of them either by burying them, even in a common container (in a properly designated cemetery), or by scattering them at sea or in a garden, forest or pond.

4. Gladys Anne Riggs is 81 years old. Her husband, George, died 10 years ago. She is retired and normally receives about $800 a month in Social Security benefits. She complains she has not received her benefits for the past 4 months. When she inquired as to the reasons for the troubles, officials at a Social Security office in your city today explained that she was dead. Four months ago, her check was returned and marked "deceased," so all her benefits were canceled. Because of the error, Mrs. Riggs fears that her check for next month may also be late, and she says she needs the money to buy food and to pay her rent. She lives alone in a one-bedroom apartment and says she has already fallen behind in her rent and is afraid she will be evicted. Social Security officials said that they will correct the problem as soon as possible and that she will receive a check for all the benefits she has missed during the past 4 months, but that it may take several weeks to issue the check. They suggested that she apply for welfare until the check arrives.

SECTION VI: LOCALIZING YOUR LEAD

INSTRUCTIONS: Write only the lead for each of the following stories.

1. The state Department of Transportation today announced plans for next year. It will spend a total of $418 million to build new roads and to improve old ones. The amount represents a $14.5 million increase over last year's total. The money comes from a state gasoline tax amounting to 4 cents per gallon sold. The department allocates the money on the basis of need, with the most congested and dangerous areas receiving the most help. Included in the allocations for next year are $17.8 million, allocated to widen from two to four lanes state highway 17-92, which runs through the southeastern part of your city for a distance of approximately three miles. Construction work on the highway project is expected to begin in four months and to be completed within one and one-half years.

2. Three persons have been killed in the crash of a single-engine plane. Police have identi-fied the victims as Mr. and Mrs. Joel Skurow of Atlanta, Georgia, and Melville Skurow of 4138 Hennessy Court in your community. Joel and Melville are brothers. The plane, flown by Joel, crashed on the outskirts of Atlanta at 7:30 a.m. today. Cause of the crash is unknown. No one on the ground was injured. Friends said Melville Skurow was visit-ing his brother, an attorney in Atlanta. Skurow is a carpenter and was thirty-seven years of age. The plane, valued at $34,800, was fully insured.

3. The annual Conference of U.S. Mayors is being held in New York City this week. Mayors from throughout the United States hold an annual convention to discuss problems of mutual interest. At the closing session today, they elected their officers for the forthcoming year, and they elected your mayor, Sabrina Datolli, first vice president. Approximately 1,460 mayors were in attendance at the convention, which next year will be held in Las Vegas.

SECTION VII: UPDATING YOUR LEAD

INSTRUCTIONS: Write only the lead for each of the following stories.

1. William MacDowell, 28, a house painter who lives at 1429 Highland Drive, is being tried for the murder of a cocktail waitress, Ethel Shearer. His trial opened last Thurs-day, and witnesses last Friday said a ring found in MacDowell's home belonged to the murder victim. MacDowell took the stand today and said he knew the victim and had bought the ring from her for $60 for a girlfriend. If convicted, MacDowell could be sentenced to life in prison. He is currently on parole after spending 8 years in prison on an armed robbery charge.

2. The state Legislature passed a law which prohibits doctors from performing abortions on girls under the age of 16 without the consent of their parents or guardians. The law specifies that doctors found guilty of violating the law can be fined up to $5,000 and can lose their licenses to practice medicine in the state. The law, which was signed by the governor, will go into effect at midnight tonight. The Legislature adopted the law after news media in the state revealed that girls as young as the age of 11 were given abortions without their parents' knowledge or consent. The law is intended to prevent that. The parents' consent must be in writing. The law stipulates that the girl who is pregnant must also agree to the abortion, so her parents cannot force her to have one unwillingly.

EXERCISE 3: Leads Pro Challenge

City, State and National Beats

INSTRUCTIONS: Write just the lead for each of the following stories. The first set of stories involves events in your city; the second set events in your state; and the third set events in the nation. A professional has been asked to write a lead for each of these stories, and the professionals' leads appear in a manual available to your instructor. You may find, however, that you like some of your own and your classmates' leads better. As you write the leads, correct the stories' spelling, style and vocabulary errors. Also, none of the possessives have been formed for you.

Name _____   Class _____   Date _____

CITY BEAT

1. Two researchers at your school today announced the results of an important study they conducted. Both are psychologists. Their study involved 50 children, all boys between the ages of ten to twelve who attend the University Learning Center. One by one, the boys were sent into a laboratory furnished to look like a playroom. They were told they could open all the drawers and look on all the shelves and play with whatever toys they found. Among the items under clothes in one drawer was a genuine pistol. The 2 researchers watched and filmed each child. One of the researchers, Aneesa Ahmadd, said many boys found the pistol and played with it and even pulled the trigger without knowing whether or not it was loaded. "They did everything from point it at each other to look down the barrel," said Prof. Ahmadd. About seventy-five percent, or 37 found the gun, and 26 handled it. At least 16 clearly pulled the trigger. Many, when questioned later, said they did not know if the gun was real. None knew it was unloaded and that the firing pin had been removed so it could not possibly be fired. All the childrens parents had given the researchers permission for their offspring to participate in the important study, and Ahmadd said many were horrified by the results, especially since all said they had warned their children never to play with guns. Ahmadd said the studys real significance is that it reveals that simple parental warnings are ineffective.

2. For the last 62 years, Olivida Saleeby has lived with her husband, Wesley, in their home at 1961 Elizabeth Lane, a structure originally built by her parents. The couple has been married all 62 of those years, immediately moving in with her parents after their honeymoon and later inheriting the house. Last week Wesley died, and his body remains unburied in a funeral home. Olivida last night asked the citys Zoning Board at its regular weekly meeting for permission to bury her dead husband in their back yard. By a vote of 7–0, board members refused. Olivida explained that she has no other living relatives, deeply loved her 81-yr.-old husband, and wanted her beloved husband to remain near her. He died suddenly and unexpectedly of a heart attack. Board members rejected her plea and explained burial in a residential neighborhood would set a bad precedent and bring down property values.

3. Susan Carigg of your city was forty-two years old and the mother of 4 kids, 3 girls and 1 boy. She was in a serious and tragic car accident 7 months ago. Since then, she's been in a coma at Mercy Hospital in your city. Her husband, Craig, now wants to remove the feeding tube that has kept his comatose spouse alive. Susans parents oppose the idea. They are Elaine and Vernon Sindelar, and they appealed to a Superior Court judge to issue an injunction to stop their son-in-law from removing the tube. The judge today ruled that Craig can proceed, clearing the way for the tubes removal by doctors. Three doctors who have treated the woman testified unanimously that she is brain dead with no hope of recovering. Mr. Carigg said he will wait until he receives final paperwork and consults again with his wifes doctors. Without the tube Mrs. Carigg will die of starvation and dehydration, probably in a period of approximately five to seven days.

4. A Circuit Court judge today issued an important decision that involves your citys school board. A gender-discrimination lawsuit was filed against the school board by girl

softball players parents. Judge McGregor ruled that the school district violated state and federal gender-discrimination laws by providing better baseball fields for boys than for girls. Two girls high school softball teams in your district have to travel up to 4 miles to practice while boys teams have fields on their high school campus. Parents complained the girls fields are unsafe and substandard, with dirty bathrooms and open-air dugouts. The judge ordered the district to bring the girls softball fields up to par with the boys fields. Like the boys fields, the new fields for the girls must have 6 foot high fencing with backstops, bleachers, dugouts with refrigerated water for each team, electronic score-boards, batting cages and 8-by-12 foot storage sheds. The School Board estimates that all that will cost approximately $600,000 to build new fields adjacent to the boys fields at the two schools involved, and the board said it does not know where the money will come from.

5. Some people in your city don't like billboards, considering them an urban blight. The issue was brought before the citys Planning Board last night. By a unanimous vote of 7–0 its members recommended banning any new billboards within the city limits and also taking down all existing billboards within seven years. Its recommendations will go to the city council for final consideration, and council members have already said they will hold two public workshops to give interested parties an opportunity to provide their input. There are currently about 180 billboards within the city. A spokesman for the citys billboard companies responded that any edict to remove existing signs is akin to stealing from legitimate businesses. She said the city government must legally pay fair market value for existing signs which are worth millions of dollars, and that local bill-board companies will sue, if necessary, to protect their property rights.

6. Deer Creek Park is normally a popular city park, but thousands of winged mammals have made their home in the rafters of the parks three picnic pavilions. People who had reserved the pavilions for picnics over the next several days have been notified the areas are now off limits. People can picnic elsewhere in the park but not in the pavilions. "In a general sense, bats are good people to have around," said Carlos Alicea, an epidemiolo-gist for the City Health Department. "They do a wonderful job of insect control, but the flip side of that is that if you have a one-on-one encounter, there could be a risk of rabies, and there's also a problem with their droppings." The city is waiting to hear from state experts about relocating the bats elsewhere in the park. One option is to erect bat houses elsewhere to provide shelter during daylight hours when the bats are inactive, but there is no guarantee the bats would use them.

STATE BEAT

1. There was a daring daylight robbery in your state capital. It involved an armored car. It was owned and operated by Brinks. Police say it is unclear whether a second person was involved, but about 400,000 dollars were taken. There were no signs of struggle or foul play, and they are looking for the trucks driver, Neil Santana, age 27. He is suspected of taking the cash while his partner went into a supermarket for a routine money pickup. He is still at large. Officials searched in and around his home and checked airports and

Name _____   Class _____   Date _____

are looking for his car. The heist occurred shortly after 4:10 p.m. yesterday afternoon when Santana drove his partner to the supermarket. As his partner went inside to pick up a bag of cash, witnesses said the driver drove off. When his partner returned, the truck was gone and remains missing. The incident occurred at the end of their route, which included a total of 22 stops and pickups. The co-worker called the police. Company officials said the driver started working for the company about five weeks ago and had no arrest record.

2. Your state legislature acted today. Its members want to end a serious problem. Each year, a dozen or more little helpless newborn babies in the state are found abandoned, and some are dead. Often, their mothers are unwed and young and don't want the babies or know how to care for their babies, so they abandon them, and some die before being found. Some mothers and some fathers kill some unwanted newborn infants. To end the problem, the legislature today adopted a law that will allow anyone to leave an unwanted newborn at any manned hospital or fire station in the state, no questions asked and with no criminal liability whatsoever. Your governor has endorsed and promised to sign the bill.

3. Jennifer Pinccus, a member of the state legislature elected from your district, is troubled. She says there are too many motor vehicle accidents, and too many of those accidents involve the elderly some of whom, according to her, "are no longer fit to drive." So she today introduced a controversial bill that would require senior motorists to take an extra test, and it is a controversial piece of legislation which will, to be passed, have to be approved by both the House and the Senate and then signed by your Governor. Under her plan, drivers age seventy-five and older would have to renew their licenses in person every three years, and would have to submit proof of hearing and vision tests by their physician when doing so. Those eighty-one and older would have to take a road test every 3 years as well as pass the screenings. Now, any driver over age seventeen can renew a six-year license two consecutive times by mail. So it is possible to hold a valid license for 18 years before having to actually walk into a state licensing bureau which Pincus thinks is too long for seniors whose health can change dramatically in a short time. Seniors are expected to actively oppose the proposal, yet 18 other states have additional testing or renewal requirements for seniors. Many require a doctors vision or hearing certification. Only 2 other states require regular road tests.

4. Your State Supreme Court decided a case today. It ruled unanimously that Jason Perez of your city can be kept in a state prison even though Perez has completed his sentence and has not been charged with a new crime. Health officials believe he is a public health risk, and a lower court judge who heard the case brought by the health officials concluded Perez cannot be trusted to participate willingly in a treatment program. So the 46-year-old tuberculosis patient sits in an isolated 6-by-10 foot cell eight days after his sentence to a state prison for assault with a deadly weapon ended and he was supposed to be a free man. His attorney wants Perez freed on his own recognizance. But before his incarceration for assault, Perez fled three times in violation of court orders and failed to get complete treatment for his drug resistant form of TB, a highly communicable and

Name _____   **Class** _____   **Date** _____

potentially deadly disease. That's why the state Dept. of Health considers him a public health risk. His attorney says he belongs in a hospital, but the Supreme Court today concurred with the lower court that he can be detained so long as he remains a clear and present health threat to others.

5. The Humane Society of your state announced today a new policy. All its city and county affiliates will immediately stop providing homeless cats to paramedic students. In the past the affiliates provided the cats so the students could practice inserting breathing tubes into humans. For as long as anyone can remember, the Humane Society allowed its city and county affiliates to provide cats scheduled to be euthanized for practice by students in emergency-medical-technician, paramedic, emergency-medical-service, and related programs. The society said it has received lots of complaints since PETA last week denounced its policy as unnecessary, gruesome, and potentially painful to the cats. People for the Ethical Treatment of Animals urged its members to withdraw all funding from the Humane Society and to encourage others to do so as well. A spokesman for the society today said no cats suffered but PETA's criticisms led to a reconsideration of the program. "We concluded there was not a need for us to be involved, and so we're out of it," she said. The cats were anesthetized but still alive when students practiced sticking breathing tubes down their throats. After the class, the cats were given a final, lethal shot. Students say they are losing an important training opportunity, especially for dealing with babies and infants, and that some young children may die since no alternatives for practicing helping them have been developed.

6. There's a new trend in your state. The population is aging, with more people over the age of 65 than ever before. So throughout your state, new hospitals are being built and old hospitals are being expanded. State health officials calculate that, across the state, the aging and inadequacy of mature buildings has fueled an unprecedented multi-billion dollar rush of construction by hospitals. Of all existing hospitals in the state, 31% are currently in the process of expanding or renovating. Two dozen of those hospitals are spending at least $25 million, and 14 are known to be spending more than $50 million each. Two dozen hospitals are enlarging crowded emergency rooms to ease overcrowding. Growing numbers of people who are uninsured or don't have family doctors go to ERs for any medical problem, sharply increasing patient volumes at ERs. Many other hospitals are expanding operating rooms, adding outpatient centers, and building physician offices to handle increased businesses. Expansions also are bringing new or larger speciality medical services such as highly profitable heart surgery centers and cancer programs needed primarily by the elderly.

NATIONAL BEAT

1. Each year the Institute for Highway Safety located in Washington D.C. gathers a variety of statistics about highway safety. It analyzes data gathered throughout the nation. Today it announced the results of a study of young drivers. It found that, of all young drivers, 16-year-old boys remain the most risky drivers on the road. 16 yr. old boys have more accidents than any other age group, and that's been true since the Institute began

analyzing highway data 32 years ago. But this year the institute found that 16-year-old girls are gaining. For every 1000 licensed 16-year-olds girls, 175 were in car accidents last year. That's up 9 percent from just 10 years ago when 160 girls crashed per 1000 drivers. Accidents for 16-year-old boys decreased slightly during the same period, from 216 to 210 per 1000 licensed drivers. A spokesman for the institute said boys are crashing less because of safer vehicle designs and less drunk driving.

2. Some men kill their wives and girlfriends. They've been the subject of a major national study. Those men typically have a long history of domestic violence. They own handguns and use them "in a final act of rage against a woman perceived to be their property," concludes the first national review of domestic violence deaths conducted by the national Centers for Disease Control. The CDC today announced that, nationally, about 19 percent of all murders are domestic related. Sixty-two percent involve the spouse or live-in girlfriend of the alleged killer. Children were the victims in roughly 11% of the cases of domestic deaths. In all, about 27% of all violent crimes reported to the FBI including murder, forcible rape, aggravated assault, and stalking involve domestic issues. And in the vast majority of cases, victims have had plenty of advance warning, as the violent behavior of their partners escalated over time. Many of those killed had received death threats from spouses who felt betrayed and jealous, the CDC concluded. Guns were the weapons of choice.

3. A startling new study shows how difficult it is to be a parent. When teens start dating new problems arise. The Harvard School of Public Health conducted a comprehensive study of 1,977 high school girls and found that 1 in 5 reported being a victim of physical or sexual violence in a dating relationship. Girls reported being hit, slapped, shoved, or forced into sexual activity by dates. Since this was the first study of its kind its not clear whether such abuse is on the rise. The report concluded that high school girls think they can handle situations they're not ready for. The researchers add that the pressures and status of having a boyfriend can propel girls into unhealthy relationships. And many of these girls never tell their moms and dads about dating violence.

4. Ralph Wick is 5 feet, 5 inches tall and weighs 342 pounds and lives in Denver. He blames fast-food restaurants for his excessive weight. He is suing 4, saying they contributed to his obesity, heart disease, and diabetes. He filed the 4 suits this week and explained at a press conference today he wants 1 million dollars from each. He is only twenty-eight years old and worked as a barber but says he's no longer able to work. He said millions of other Americans also should sue the companies which sell products loaded with saturated fats, trans fats, salt, cholesterol, and other harmful dietary content. He says he wants to warn everyone of the adverse health effects that could cause obesity, diabetes, heart disease, high blood pressure, and elevated cholesterol levels. A spokesman for McDonalds, one of the companies he's suing, called the suit "frivolous." The other restaurants he's suing include Pizza Hut, Wendys, and Burger King, since he says he ate at them an average of once or more a day.

5. Kimberley Mchalik, one of Harvards most prominent Sociologists, focuses on marriage and family life as her primary area of study. Today she spoke to 6000 delegates

attending the national convention of the Association of University Women in San Francisco and said: "As women age, more and more who never married or lose a spouse complain there are no good men left. But instead of griping, women should increase their pool of prospects. As women become more successful, independent, and confident, they're better able to dump societys old rules and create new ones. No longer are younger men out of the question. Each generation becomes more tolerant and progressive. Plus, men usually are the ones putting the moves on older women. What attracts them are the older womens accomplishments, sophistication, and self-assurance. And the fact that older women are looking much younger. You've got to realize that women now take much better care of themselves. We eat more healthfully, go to the gym, and spend more time taking care of ourselves. Sure, there can be problems. If the age difference is more than 10 or 15 years, it becomes a little edgy. As you approach a decades difference, you have men and women born in different social contexts that affect their attitudes about marriage and relationships. Whether these relationships work out generally depends on the individuals involved. Couples need to share common values and to figure out whether they're at the same stage of life. Differences in incomes, the desire for children, and decisions about when to retire can be problems. But couples who iron out those differences can go the distance."

Name _____ Class _____ Date _____

EXERCISES TO ACCOMPANY CHAPTER **8**

Alternative Leads

EXERCISE 1: **Evaluating Alternative Leads**

INSTRUCTIONS: Critically evaluate the following leads, each of which uses one of the alternative forms discussed in the "Alternative Leads" chapter of the text. Select the best leads and explain why they succeed. Point out the flaws in the remaining leads. As you evaluate the leads, look for lessons—"do's and don'ts"— that you can apply to your own work.

1. A new shopping center will bring 11,000 jobs, millions of dollars in tax revenue, offices, and a residential area.
   Critics fear it will also bring crime, traffic, and pollution, destroying their quiet way of life.

2. Should elderly drivers be tested more frequently?

3. People in shorts and T-shirts packed the courtroom. They appeared relaxed at first and perhaps slightly annoyed at being summoned to court.
   Circuit Court Judge JoAnn Kaeppler took her seat and began asking the visitors, one by one, why they failed to pay the court costs and fines she had imposed as punishment for crimes such as drunken driving and theft.
   The courtroom visitors grew visibly worried as Kaeppler, 44, sternly continued.
   Some visitors frowned. Others fingered their wallets.
   They had figured it out. If they didn't have the money, they were going to jail. Immediately! Right then!

4. Retirement may be hazardous to your health.

5. As the foreman's verdict of "innocent" echoed through the courtroom Tuesday, Jim Picott wiped the tears from his eyes and hugged his defense attorney. In the back of the room Marilyn Boudinot stomped out of the courtroom, slamming the door behind her.

6. Are you missing any jewelry?

7. It's 8 a.m., do you know where your cat is? You may need to check.

8. The suspect tore through a homeowner's fence, ripped down a clothesline with his teeth, slammed head-on into a travel trailer, then bolted down the street.

9. Police had a description of the offender: Male, black hair, brown eyes, 715 pounds.

10. Four years ago Christine Belcuor went to a doctor to have an annual check-up that included a mammogram. Eight months later doctors informed her that she had breast cancer.

Name _____   Class _____   Date _____

Tuesday afternoon Mrs. Belcuor and her husband, Paul, testified against five doctors for failure to detect cancer in her breast.

11. Is the City Council putting the cart before the horse by depending on a $100,000 grant from the State Recreation Development Assistance program?

12. "It was a dumb mistake, I admit it. But I didn't hurt anyone but myself, and I don't think I should have to go to jail." Those were the words today of a 20-year-old accused arsonist.

13. A petition signed by all 23 students in a philosophy class calls their faculty member a tyrant who "cursed, insulted and intimidated students, causing some to cry and others to flee."

14. Alex Rue wonders if he will ever find work in the city.
The 30-year-old college graduate with a business degree spends most of his day in an unemployment office browsing help-wanted ads.
"I haven't found anything yet," he said in disgust. "This city has a lot of job openings if you want to work as a clerk at a convenience store. But I didn't spend five years of my life in college so I could sweep floors or pump gas for $5 an hour."
Rue's concerns about finding solid employment in the city are common. Many skilled workers who faced the same dilemma have left and found higher paying jobs elsewhere in the state.

15. Boom! Beep, beep, beep, beep, boom!
These are the repetitive sounds outside campus dorms every weekday, starting as early as 6 a.m. The shrill sound of jackhammers pierces the quiet air; lumbering front-end loaders haul away debris; foremen shout orders to dirt-covered workmen, hammering, digging, scraping. All in the name of progress.

16. Have you ever looked around your classrooms and thought that older women students have advantages over students just out of high school? If so, is it because they seem more interested in what is going on in class, or is it because we think they have more time on their hands than the rest of us?

17. After 17 years with the city, police chief Barry Kopperud is hanging up his holster.

EXERCISE 2: Writing Alternative Leads

INSTRUCTIONS: Using techniques you studied in this chapter, write an alternative lead for each of the following stories. You may want to use complete or partial quotations, questions, descriptions, buried leads, multiparagraph leads, suspense, or chronological order. Or you may want to try a shocking lead, ironic lead, direct-address lead, or a word used in an unusual way.

1. It's a startling announcement for many. Made today by people at the United States Department of Agriculture in Washington, D.C. The topic? The cost of raising a baby. The department surveyed 12,850 families with two parents and also a total of 3,395

Name _____ Class _____ Date _____

single-parent households. It asked parents about the cost of raising a typical child from birth to age 17. Parents calculated housing was the biggest expense, totaling $49,710 in cost over that period of years. Food was the second greatest expense, at an average total cost of $26,130, followed closely by transportation, clothing, and child care. Viewed another way, on an annual basis, it now costs about $8,300 a year or $694 a month to raise one child in a two-child, two-parent, middle-income family, the survey found. The total cost for a child in that environment is $149,820. By comparison, today's grandparents paid one-sixth that much. Several expenses, such as child care, weren't a factor in earlier times. In 1960, the first year the department conducted the survey, the total cost of raising a child was $25,229. Prices are higher in West Coast cities, followed by East Coast cities. Midwestern cities and rural areas are the least expensive places to raise children.

2. James "J.J." Jones is a cab driver in your city. Well after midnight one Saturday night three months ago, he saw two young men standing outside a bar that is a popular college campus drinking spot. Both young men are 21 years of age and students at your institution. They had been drinking beer and talking to their pals. They wanted to move on to an apartment where they thought a good party was going on. They waved down Jones's cab, which stopped. When the cab reached their destination, they jumped and ran, going in different directions. But Jones, also a student at your school and a member of its track team, wasn't going to be cheated. He proceeded to jump out of the car and chase the men. As Jones got closer, one cheat stumbled on a curb and fell. Jones grabbed him and they rolled on the pavement and threw a few punches, apparently doing little harm. This altercation was all witnessed by a couple of female students who happened to be driving by and phoned for the police, not knowing what the commotion was all about. Before the police arrived, Jones won the wrestling match and wound up sitting on top and demanding payment, but when the cheat said he was broke and showed him his empty wallet, Jones noticed that the cheat was wearing a wristwatch. Jones said he would take the watch, turn it into his manager, and the cheat could get it back when he shows up and pays for the ride. After taking the watch, Jones left with a few hours left to work. After work he turned in the watch. Meanwhile, the police arrived at the scene and found the student sitting on the pavement, moaning in pain, as he had apparently broken his ankle when he tripped. He said the cab driver beat him up, but he declined to bring an assault charge, only a robbery charge. The young man later talked to a lawyer. The law says the cab driver should not have chased the young man for his money and had no right to touch him. He could only call for a cop or go to a police station and report the incident. The young man subsequently said it was J.J.'s fault he broke his ankle and suffered pain. He sued the cab company. The cab company lawyers decided today to settle for $16,500, and the cab driver had to dig into his own pocket for about $1,000 to cover his own legal fees. As part of the settlement, the young man agreed to drop a criminal charge of robbery, a serious felony, which he filed against J.J., accusing him of using force and violence to take his watch without his permission.

3. Melbi Novogroski is a resident of your city and happier today than yesterday. Yesterday her jewelry mistakenly and somehow accidentally went out in the trash. Melbi and her

husband, Harry R., scoured the city dump for four hours until they found the red velvet pouch holding a diamond-studded platinum ring, other rings, bracelets, and chains. "The thing that was so important in that jewelry was my grandmother's ring," said Melba to you. "No dollar amount would ever replace the sentimental value." A call to the city Sanitation Department led the couple to the truck on their route, and everyone met at the dump for the smelly search. The driver "tried to guess where approximately our garbage would be," Melba said. The truck crew, dump workers, and the couple waded in to help, and the landfill foreman narrowed the search by suggesting people check envelope addresses to get close to the couple's home. Finally, the baseball-sized pouch was found by Melba herself. "Gee, the shower felt good when we got home," Harry said.

4. Cats are a wonderful household pet and now the No. 1 favorite pet in the country. More homes have cats than dogs. Now, however, environmentalists say they're a threat to wildlife. There are millions of cats in this state alone, especially on farms. In some areas of the state, cats outnumber all other native mammalian predators combined. Kitties kill hundreds of millions of animals, and that certainly includes tens of millions of young, little, helpless song birds as well as more rabbits than hunters bag every year. Grassland birds are in particular danger because their pasture habitats are usually within hunting range of farm cats. In addition, felines compete for prey with other predators. If rabbits and mice are being eaten by cats, that means there is less to eat for native predators such as hawks and owls. Cats are an important ecological factor nationwide. In southern states, where many domesticated felines have gone wild, they're having tremendous problems with cat predators on wildlife. In the Southwest, cats that venture forth into the desert are basically decimating the small lizard populations; the furry creatures don't need to be hungry to hunt because their instinct is to kill even if they are full.

5. Police stopped and arrested 44 drivers driving more than 30 mph down Wacker Road last week. Neighbors had repeatedly complained to the police and other city officials, including to members of the city council, about speeders in their residential neighborhood, and police responded with beefed-up patrols. So for all of last week, police went about ticketing drivers for speeding over 30 mph along a 3-mile stretch of the road. Today police are embarrassed. The speed limit is 45 mph, not 30. Someone apparently replaced at least one of the 45 mph speed limit signs on the road with a 30 mph sign. The prankster may never be found. Motorists, however, complained. "I was going 44 when I got pulled over," said one. "I didn't expect to get a ticket. I've been driving that road for years, and everyone here knows it's a 45 zone." Judge Marci Hall said she has been contacted by the police: asked to dismiss all 44 speeding tickets, and that she is in the process of doing so. The sign was an official sign apparently stolen from elsewhere and erected in secret, probably at night by a person or persons unknown. After the sign was put up, people began complaining that drivers were violating the 30 mph speed limit, so police went out to Wacker Road and began stopping motorists. The prankster would likely face criminal mischief charges if caught.

6. You interviewed a police officer in your city, Lieutenant Alvin Innis, who is in charge of the police department's Vehicle Theft Division. He told you: "So many professional

criminals have taken up auto theft that the chance of recovering a stolen car has declined to little better than 50–50 and locking your car provides less protection than ever. Vehicle theft is no longer a matter of juvenile joyriding. People under age 18 accounted for 56 percent of the vehicle thieves arrested 20 years ago but only 40 percent last year. This is increasingly becoming an adult crime involving gangs—professionals— making enormous profits." Increasing adult involvement, increasing thefts of trucks and commercial vehicles, and declining recovery rates are strong indicators that vehicular theft has become the province of professional criminals. Last year autos accounted for only 75 percent of the vehicles stolen in your city; trucks and buses 14 percent and motorcycles and other vehicles 11 percent. At the same time, the recovery rate dropped from 84 percent 20 years ago to 55 percent last year. Four out of five stolen autos were unlocked, and one in five had the key left in the ignition. Thieves can take or sell these vehicles to chop shops that strip them in a couple hours, then sell the parts. "Once they're cut up, it's almost impossible to find them," Lieutenant Innis went on by saying and concluding.

EXERCISE 3: Writing Alternative Leads—Pro Challenge

INSTRUCTIONS: Professionals have written alternative leads for the following stories. Write an alternative lead for each of the stories. When you finish, you can compare your work with that of the professionals. Their leads appear in a manual available to your instructor. You may find, however, that you like some of your own and your classmates' leads better.

1. In many ways, it was a rather common robbery. Fortunately, the police succeeded in capturing the apparent perpetrator. This is the story. Employees at the First Union Bank, 3720 Kohlar Boulevard, pushed an alarm button at 2:38 p.m. yesterday after a lone man came into the bank and demanded money. The man said he had a sawed-off shotgun under his raincoat. A teller gave him money in a paper bag he carried. She also slipped in an exploding dye pack. Just as the man left the bank the pack detonated, and the man tossed the bag containing the money into the bushes. Witnesses said he fled on foot. Officers started combing the area, looking for a man in a yellow shirt, blue jeans, and raincoat. They lifted the lid of a trash bin behind the McDonald's at 3782 Kohlar Boulevard and found him there. He was crouched among the half-eaten burgers and fries. Police identified him as Alan Franklin, age 23, of 820 Apollo Drive, Apartment #223.

2. Judge Samuel McGregor performed the unusual wedding Monday. He married Sunni McGrath and Wallace A. Svec. It wasn't a fancy wedding. There was no cake or dress or hugs, not even a kiss. They weren't allowed. Why? Because McGregor performed the wedding in his courtroom, minutes after sentencing McGrath to a year's probation for drunken driving. Immediately after the wedding ceremony, the bride was ordered back to prison. She is serving time there for other crimes. Thus their honeymoon will be delayed. "It was real different. But I feel really good because I love him to death," McGrath said from her jail cell yesterday afternoon. The two have dated for three years and said they wanted to marry to avoid problems with prison visitation rights and requirements. McGrath is scheduled to be released in three months, and the couple

has plans for a traditional wedding—flower girl and all—at that time. At yesterday's ceremony, a blue jail uniform served as her wedding gown. For security reasons—so they could not pass anything to one another (notes, drugs, weapons, or anything)—an attorney stood between the couple as they exchanged vows. The couple longed to kiss. The judge suggested they wave instead. They did. They also blew kisses. McGrath said she planned to spend her wedding night watching television. Svec wasn't certain what he would do. Because McGrath was already on probation for burglary, grand theft and possession of cocaine, the arrest for drunken driving resulted in her being returned to jail. She said she committed the other crimes to support a drug habit that she said she has kicked.

3. It was 12:40 a.m. today, and the incident occurred at a home located at 4772 E. Harrison Ave. Two men were involved: Michael Uosis and Edward Beaumont, 40. Uosis lives in the home and, a few weeks ago, was robbed. This morning Uosis heard someone banging at a window of his home. He thought it was the man who had robbed him, coming back to rob him again. So Uosis went to a closet, got out a .38-caliber revolver, and fired a single shot at the window. Uosis said he didn't see anyone and didn't mean to shoot anyone and only fired the gun to scare away whoever was outside. "I didn't mean to shoot him," Uosis said. "He was a good friend, and I didn't know it was him outside. I didn't even see who it was outside." Neither the police nor Uosis know why Beaumont, who used to work with Uosis, both as postal workers, until Uosis retired three years ago, had gone to the house at 12:40 a.m. Beaumont is in serious condition in the intensive care unit at Regional Medical Center. Hospital officials said Beaumont may be paralyzed as a result of the gunshot wound to his head. Police charged Uosis with aggravated battery, and he was released from the city jail after posting $2,500 bail. If convicted, he could be sentenced to as much as 15 years in prison and fined up to $10,000. Under state law, it is illegal for a resident to use unnecessary force against an intruder unless the resident is defending himself or another occupant of the home against death or great bodily harm.

4. There was another burglary in the city. A pair of burglars struck VFW Post #40 at 640 Sherwood Drive. Both burglars appeared to be teenagers. Janitor Steven Cowles heard them. Cowles, age 70, didn't catch them, however. He said, "I'm getting old, and it would have been a chore catching up with them. They lit out." Cowles went to work at the VFW post at about 5 a.m. today and almost tripped and fell over two knapsacks filled with expensive liquor and cigarettes from the post. "I knew something was funny. Then here's those two kids coming around the corner by the popcorn machine," he said. "I let out a big noise and said a few things. I had two loaves of stale bread for the ducks I feed every morning and an old box of Entenmann's sticky buns. I started hitting them with the bread, and then I threw the buns at them. That's when they dropped everything and ran. I went to a phone and called the cops."

5. The drama started when Lillian Sodergreen parked her car and ran into the supermarket to buy a gallon of milk and other groceries. She told her son in the back seat to sit still and be quiet while she was gone. Her daughter was already sleeping.

Name _____   **Class** _____   **Date** _____

She said it is the last time she will leave the children alone. The admitted criminal is Troy Dusart, 21. Troy is a car thief and admits it. He insists, however, that he is not a kidnapper. He wanted a car to steal for a joy-ride and, at approximately 8:30 a.m. Tuesday, noticed a car left running, with the keys in the ignition, parked outside a supermarket: Albertsons at 4240 Michigan Street. Normally, he's careful. "There are rules to follow," he explained in an interview with you in his cell in the city jail. "My number one rule is: 'Make sure you don't get more than you bargained for.'" But he was "moving too fast," he said. So he didn't see the children in the back seat: Troy Sodergreen, age 4, and his little sister, Jena, age 8 months. "I saw the keys and got in, but I didn't notice the kids," he continued. He peeled out of the supermarket parking lot. "When I turned around the corner, I looked to my side and saw the little girl lying on the seat, and then another kid. I saw the kids and say, 'Oh, damn.' I freaked out and parked the car." Dysart is now charged with grand theft and kidnapping. He added, "I didn't want nothing to do with the kids. I didn't touch the kids. My wife has three kids. I don't need no more kids. I'm going to tell the judge the same thing. He can charge me, but I didn't know they were there. Why would I want more kids?" The children were unharmed.

EXERCISES TO ACCOMPANY CHAPTER **9**

The Body of a News Story

EXERCISE 1: The Body of a News Story

SECTION I: SECOND PARAGRAPHS

INSTRUCTIONS: Second paragraphs are almost as important as leads. Like leads, second paragraphs must help arouse readers' interest in a topic. Critically evaluate the second paragraphs in the following stories. Judge which of the second paragraphs are most successful in (1) providing a smooth transition from the lead; (2) continuing to discuss the topic summarized in the lead; and (3) emphasizing the news—details that are new, important and interesting. Give each second paragraph a grade from A to F.

1. A Pinkerton courier was robbed at gunpoint and fatally wounded on Tuesday while leaving Merchants Bank with the day's daily transaction records.

   Edwin James, 59, of 826 Bell Drive, was following standard bank procedures and carrying no money. (Grade: _____)

2. A 41-year-old teacher who fell and broke an ankle while stopping for a cup of coffee on her way to work sued a convenience store Monday.

   The teacher, Tina Alvarez, has worked at Washington Elementary School for 21 years. (Grade: _____)

3. Two young men are presumed dead after falling off a 30-foot rock formation into the Pacific Ocean at a California park Saturday.

   The men remain unidentified, and their bodies have not been recovered. (Grade: _____)

4. Police responding to a 911 call about a shooting at 10 p.m. Sunday discovered Ralph Beasley on Bennett Road with a gunshot wound to his head.

   County sheriff's deputies arrived at about the same time in response to a radio request for assistance. An ambulance was already at the scene, as were Fire Department paramedics. (Grade: _____)

5. A 32-year-old woman who said she smoked marijuana to ease the pain of a rare intestinal disease was charged Tuesday morning with possessing illegal drugs.

   Ruth Howland was stopped at the Municipal Airport after a K-9 dog singled out her suitcase. She and her husband, Terry, were returning from Mexico. (Grade: _____)

6. Three gunmen who entered a restaurant on Wilson Avenue at 10:30 p.m. Tuesday held four employees and 12 customers at gunpoint while taking more than $3,000 from several cash registers.

   Peggy Deacosti, the restaurant's hostess, was on duty when the robbery occurred. (Grade: _____)

Name _____   Class _____   Date _____

7. Eileen Guion, 38, a food and beverage coordinator at Walt Disney World for 18 years, died at her home Tuesday of unknown causes.

   Although she was offered many other jobs at restaurants, she never accepted them. She once said, "I've loved working at Disney because I get to work with people from all over the world, and I think that is very neat." (Grade: _____)

8. Police are searching for a man who attacked a woman outside the Bayside Bar & Grill Thursday night.

   Terry Smythe, a bartender at the restaurant, said he heard a woman screaming outside the entrance at 9 p.m. Smythe darted to the foyer, where he saw the woman trapped in the entryway. Smythe said it was "kind of like a tug of war," with the assailant trying to pull the woman outside while waitresses tried to pull her inside. (Grade: _____)

SECTION II: TRANSITIONS

INSTRUCTIONS: Critically evaluate the following transitions. Which would be most likely to entice you to continue reading the stories? Which provide a smooth, specific, informative and interesting introduction to the next idea? Give each transition a grade from A to F.

1. _____ Other students said they would tell their teachers about cheaters because cheating is not fair to those who take the time to study.

2. _____ But what should happen when a husband and wife disagree about having a baby?

3. _____ A concerned citizen then addressed the commission about the fence.

4. _____ Next, the Task Force presented its plan for preservation and renovation of the downtown.

5. _____ In a flat, emotionless voice, Howard responded that he and Jackson stole a red Mustang convertible on the night of June 3, picked up the two 14-year-old girls, and took them to the motel.

6. _____ Gary Hubbard, superintendent of schools, then addressed his concerns about security in the city's schools.

7. _____ Police Chief Barry Kopperud said his department is trying to combat juvenile crime by changing the way officers interact with children.

8. _____ He then discussed prejudice as a problem that plagues society.

9. _____ She also spoke about the different religious celebrations and rituals.

10. _____ Parents who love, care for and respect their children don't raise delinquents, she said.

Name _____   Class _____ Date _____

EXERCISE 2: The Body of a News Story: Pro Challenge
Writing Complete News Stories

INSTRUCTIONS: Write complete news stories based on the following information. Be thorough and use most of the information provided. Because much of the material is wordy, awkward and poorly organized, you will have to rewrite it extensively. Correct all errors in your rewrite. When you finish, you can compare your work to a professional's. Experienced reporters have been asked to write stories for each set of facts, and their work appears in a manual available to your instructor.

1. A family that owns a farm about 2 miles outside your town has decided to sell it. It has been in they're family for four generations. They often bring fresh eggs, produce and other items to the farmers market in town to sell, which is held once a month on the first Saturday. The father of the family told you they are selling because their children are nearly grown and don't want to farm, and that they will be moving to another state to be closer to other family members, but he declined to say any more than that. A real estate developer is buying the property, and he wants to subdivide it for single-family homes and town houses. There would be a total of five hundred new homes as the developer, Eugene McIntry, President of McIntry Realty, has planned it. McIntery has submitted his subdivision plan to the county commissioners. The commissioners and the County Planning Commission are extremely worried about this giant new development. They don't believe their roads and their water and sewer systems can handle all those people. In fact, right now the water system and sewer system don't even run to the farm. The family that lives on the farm have a well and a septic tank for their house and another well for their barn. But, the county doesn't have any zoning, so the supervisors don't think they can keep McIntry from buying the farm and building all those homes. Plus, McIntry has threatened to file a lawsuit if the township tries anything to keep his plans from going through. He said he has a lot of money invested and doesn't want to lose it. Some nearby residents, however, are going to file a lawsuit of their own to keep him from building the houses. They are angry that they're peaceful, quiet stretch of road just outside the city will soon be filled with cars and their view will be ruined by hundred's of new houses. The residents attorney, Hector Salvatore, says he is finishing up the suit and will file it in County Court next week. He said the residents also are afraid they will be forced to hook up to the water and sewer systems if they are expanded out to the farm, which means several hundred dollars out of each of their pockets, which he said is unfair and possibly illegal.

2. A bad accident happened this morning on the intestate highway that runs right along the western edge of your city. It is Interstate 790. Apparently two tractor trailers collided and started a chain reaction crash. The citys Police Department is not done investigating the accident, which happened at 6:45 a.m. in the morning, but that is what they believe preliminarily. A total of 4 tractor-trailers and fourteen cars were involved, according to Sgt. Albert Wei of the police department. One of the tractor-trailers was a tanker hauling diesel fuel; it was very lucky, Wei said, that it didn't roll over or dump any fuel or catch fire. The truck part of the tanker was

damaged when a car hit it, but the truck driver managed to get it stopped along the side of the road. He wasn't hurt, Wei said, but 2 people driving cars were killed and twenty other people were injured and taken to the hospital, four of them seriously hurt. The fire chief, Tony Sullivan, said those seriously hurt people had injuries that were life-threatening. One of the ambulance drivers told him that. Sulluvan said his firefighters had to cut the roofs off three of the cars to free the drivers and passengers that were trapped inside. All five of the fire department's ambulances were on the seen, along with ambulances from four nearby citys' fire departments. Also, the "Life Flight" helicopter from Memorial Hospital in you're city was called to the scene and flew two of the worst injuries to the trauma center in Statesville, 50 miles away. Sullivan said the crash scene looked like something from a war zone when he arrived, with bodies laying along the road, people covered with blood sitting next to their cars, emergency workers running from place to place trying to help the injured, and sirens wailing in the distance as more fire trucks and ambulances were called. He had never seen anything that bad in the 18 and a half years he's been with the fire department. Wie said the police officers on the scene were having trouble figuring out which people were from which vehicles, and who were the drivers and who were the passengers. According to Wei, the accident, which happened in the northbound lanes, closed the entire highway, north and south. The interstate was still closed at 10 a.m., the deadline for your story, and Wei had no idea when it would be open again.
It created quite a mess for the rush hour traffic today, since people who normally would have used Interstate 790 had to go on Interstate 690, on the eastern side of the city, and that backed up traffic on 690 for three hours.

3. It seems to be turning into a controversy in your local school district. The School Board is considering implementing random drug testing of all student athletes at the high school. Students and parents on both sides of the issue plan to attend tomorrow night's board meeting, which was to be in the library at Wilson Elementary School but has been moved to the cafeteria at Kennedy High School to accommodate the expected large audience. The 5 school board members you were able to talk to this morning before your deadline, David DeBecker, Mimi Lieber, Judie Lu, Diana Maceda and Jane Tribitt, were reluctant to say anything before the meeting that might give away their positions on the issue. Gary Hubbard is the Superintendent of schools. He didn't really want to say much either when you called him, but then did admit that he was the one who asked the board to consider the new policy. He believes there are members of the football and boys basketball teams that are using steroids and other performance-enhancing drugs, and said some players on those teams have come to him and complained. The school can't test only certain athletes, Hubberd said, so they have to test players in all sports. DeBecker referred you to the school boards attorney, Karen Bulnes. She said she has drafted a proposed policy for the board to consider, but said she doesn't know how they will vote. She said such a policy is legal based on past United States Supreme Court decisions. You were able to talk to some students at the high school this morning before classes started. Hazel Beaumont was dropping off her son, Roger, in front of the school. Roger is a tenth-grader who is playing soccer this fall. He thinks drug testing is a

violation of his privacy, but then admitted that he really likes playing soccer and probably would take the test. His mother said she would make him take the test, and said she'll be at the school board meeting. Two girls who play field hockey, Ann Capiello and Amy Deacosti, don't like the idea either, but said they don't have anything to hide and would take the test if required. Both girls are seniors, and when you asked them about the football players taking steroids, Ann said she has heard that. James Carigg and Diana Nyer are seniors who both play basketball, and both are opposed to drug testing. In fact, they plan to go to the meeting and voice they're opinions against the idea. Lu called you back after you had talked with her and said she decided to publicly say that she is in favor of the idea because she thinks it will be a deterrent for students who might be thinking about taking drugs. The meeting will start at 7 p.m.

4. Fire destroyed two businesses downtown last night, and police think it was arson. They also think they know who set the fire, which caused an estimated five hundred thousand dollars' damage. The businesses that were destroyed were Kalani Brothers Bakery and Barton School of Dance. The fire started in the bakery and spread to the dance studio. Fire chief Tony Sullivan said an automatic alarm at the bakery sounded at 11:35 p.m. When the first fire truck arrived on the scene, flames were shooting out the front of the bakery, where a large picture window had burst, and fire was visible on the 2nd floor, where the dance studio was located. The city fire department was assisted by fire companies from two neighboring towns. A total of 75 firemen and other emergency personnel responded to the call. The first fireman on the scene was Eddy Muldaur, a student at Lake Community College and a volunteer with the city fire department. He told you last night at the scene that there was a lot of smoke and flames coming from the building when he got there. About ten minutes later, the first truck arrived. You were very surprised this morning to find out that Police chief Barry Kopperud issued a news release saying that Muldaur had been arrested and charged with arson for allegedly setting the fire and damaging the sprinkler system so it wouldn't work. He was placed in the city jail on $1 million dollars bail. Eileen Barton, the owner of Barton School of Dance, was inconsolable when you talked to her this morning. She started the dance school 8 years ago. It was the only thing she ever wanted to do. She invested all her savings to start the school; that was the money that her grandfather left her when he died. She has no idea what she'll due because she doesn't think her insurance payment will be enough to start over. The president of the Kalani Brother's Bakery, Charles Kalani said he and his brother, Andrew, will re-open eventually, but in a different location, although he didn't know where yet. He was very angry to learn that the fire had been started intentionally. The two businesses were located at 338 North Fifteenth St. It took firefighters 1 and a half hours to get the fire under control. A business in the building next door, at 340 North Fifteenth Street, Bon Voyage Travel Agency, suffered some smoke and water damage. The manager there, Wayne Morell, said they would be closed today but hoped to open again tomorrow. Chief Sullivan said he found gasoline soaked rags in the back room of the bakery, which they believe were used to start the fire. When he heard that Muldaur was the first one on the scene, he said, he was

Name _____ **Class** _____ **Date** _____

surprised because he lives on the other side of the city, further away than the fire companys headquarters. Police found a can of gas and a bag of rags in Eddy's pick-up truck. No one was in the building at the time of the fire, and no one was injured fighting it.

5. A magic act at an outdoor childrens festival in your city over the weekend turned out to be no treat for 3 youngsters that had to be taken to the hospital after they were scratched by a rabbit who then disappeared into some bushes. The children were started on a series of rabies shots just to be sure they weren't infected by the rabbit, which could not be found. The magic act was performed by Maggie the Magician, who travels to festivals through out the state with her act, which is aimed at little children and includes small animals like rabbits and turtles that the children can touch and hold. Maggie said nothing like this had ever happened before in the 4 and a half years she's been doing her act. The accident came at the end of her act, when she made the big white rabbit in question, who she called Buster, appear out of a tophat. The children watching her act gathered around to pet Buster when he apparently was frightened by a baby's crying and tried to get away. The 3 children he scratched tried to grab Buster but couldn't hold on. Harriet Ruiz, Director of Public Affairs at Regional Medical Center, where the 3 youths were taken for treatment, said they will have to have two additional shots unless the rabbit is found and it can be determined that it is not rabid. She declined to give you they're names, but said 2 of the 3 were brother and sister, ages 5 and 4, respectively, and the other was a four-year-old boy. Kim Rybinski, owner of Kim's Pets, who sells rabbits along with numerous other small animals, said it was highly unlikely that Buster had rabies because he was in captivity and never got exposed to wild animals. Michael Jeffreys, director of the Humane Society, said several society volunteers helped Maggie search for Buster, but to no avail. He agreed with Rybinksi that Buster probably didn't have rabies, but said you can't take chances with someone's life. Maggie was uncertain how Buster would survive by himself, but said she had to leave to go to another festival the next day. The festival was held from 10 a.m. to 2 p.m. Saturday at the city park. Maggie's act was on from 10:30 to 10:45. The children were taken by their parents to the hospital right after the accident. A paramedic from the city ambulance department, Julius Povacz, who was volunteering at the festival, cleaned up the children's scratches and advised the parent's to take them to the hospital. He said the wounds were minor. Just as you are approaching deadline on your story, you get a call from Emil Plambeck, Superintendent of the city parks commission. A city worker, Carlos Alicea, was picking up trash in the park this morning when he spotted Buster sitting under a tree and captured him. Now Buster can be quarantined and checked for rabies, and the children hopefully can avoid furthur shots, Ruiz said when you called her back.

6. Your State Legislature is considering a bill that would change the state law requiring motorcyclists to wear helmets. Many physicians in your city are opposed to the bill. About fifty of them held a press conference yesterday afternoon. They unveiled

a petition to legislators asking them not to pass the bill. Doctors from Memorial Hospital, Mercy Hospital, Regional Medical Center, Sacred Heart Hospital, St. Nicholas Hospital and the Medi-First Clinic were present at the press conference. In the audience also were over a hundred nurses, paramedics and other healthcare professionals supporting the doctors. The press conference was held on the front lawn of Memorial Hospital, the largest of the citys hospitals, and while it was going on, 2 ambulances came racing into the parking lot and pulled up to the Emergency Room doors with victims from a two-vehicle accident. Ironically, one of the victims injured in the accident had been on a motorcycle. The doctors have gotten nearly four hundred signatures so far on they're petition and hope to have at least five hundred by the time they send it to the legislature. The number of serious head injuries caused by motorcycle accidents in your state is over 70% less now then when the helmet law was adopted 25 years ago, according to Dr. Karl Sodergreen. He said that reduction is directly related to passage of that law. Dr. Hector Rivera said a study from last year about health-care costs related to motorcycle riding by the state medical society showed that emergency room costs alone could go up by more than 45 percent if the helmet law is repealed. The motorcyclist injured in the accident was 19-year-old Grady Smith of 8213 Peach Street. Smith suffered a broken arm and several broken ribs. In the report from city police, his doctor was quoted as saying Smiths injuries would have been much worse if he had not been wearing a helmet. Dr. Sodergreen said the physicians plan to send their petition to the legislature on Monday. The bill is to be considered by the Legislature next Wednesday.

EXERCISE 3: The Body of a News Story

Writing Complete News Stories

INSTRUCTIONS: Write complete news stories based on the following information. Critically examine the information's language and organization, improving it whenever possible. To provide a pleasing change of pace, use quotations in your stories. Go beyond the superficial; unless your instructor tells you otherwise, assume that you have enough space to report every important and interesting detail. Correct all errors.

1. Your county's Industrial Development Authority made an announcement today. A local company that manufactures automobile parts received a $250,000 grant to retrain some of its workers. The training is required because the company won a contract with the United States government to manufacture replacement parts for military vehicles. The money was provided through your state's Critical Job Training program. The program was designed two years ago to help keep critical and high-paying manufacturing jobs in the state. State and county officials had said too many manufacturing jobs were leaving the state. Only about 16 percent of the jobs in the state involve manufacturing. The rest are professional, service-related or agricultural jobs. The company receiving the training funds is TCB Manufacturing Company Incorporated. The money will allow the company to train 50 current employees, as well as the 150 additional employees that will be hired to work on the

new contract. The training will begin next month and continue for 8 to ten weeks. TCB is one of the largest manufacturing companies in your county, employing nearly 2,500 workers at two plants in the county. TCB recently recalled 300 workers that had been laid off last year because of the downturn in the economy that had affected car sales. TCB manufactures high-quality steering gear, transmission and brake assembly parts for several automotive manufacturers. "These training funds will help 50 of our employees to keep their jobs and will enable us to hire 150 new people. This program is a benefit for the people of this county and the state and shows how government and business can work together to improve the economy," said TCB vice president of human resources Jonathan Seiler. At one time TCB employed nearly 4,000 people in manufacturing, but the introduction of robotic welding and assembly machines three years ago eliminated some jobs. "This training program will give me a new lease on my work life. Without it I might have been laid off because I don't have the skills necessary to run the new machines needed for this new contract we got from the military. I would never be able to find another job in the county with the pay and benefits that this job has," said Frank Peacock. Peacock has worked for TCB for 25 years. He is 47 and went to work for TCB after serving four years in the Army. "These funds will allow TCB to remain a major economic force in the county. Keeping manufacturing jobs is important to the local community, the state and our country," said state Representative Constance Wei. Wei was at the 11 a.m. press conference announcing the awarding of the grant. Wei helped the county apply for the money and worked with state officials to get the funds approved.

2. Researchers at the U.S. Department of Health and Human Services are puzzled. A report released Monday in Washington, D.C., by the U.S. Census was unexpected, researchers said. The census is collected every ten years. The last one was in 2010. The Census Bureau data shows that median income for a single-parent household run by a mother is about $25,000. The median income for a single-parent household headed by a father is $35,000. Yet HHS researchers found that children in single-father households are more likely not to have health insurance. Researchers found that 40% of the 2.5 million single-parent families headed by the father had children without health coverage while only 19% of the 4.9 million single-parent households headed by the mother had children without coverage. Researchers found that only 12 percent of the nation's 10.8 million married couple homes had children without health care coverage. HHS spokesman Jenna Olivetti declined to speculate during Monday's press conference on any government action regarding the trend. She did comment on what she thought may be causing it. "This is something we have never seen before in our research. I'm wondering if single-dad households are less aware of the help they can get from public programs that are available to them," Olivetti said. In the one million homes where a single father raised two or more children, nearly 20 percent had all children uninsured compared to just 10% of the single-mother households with two or more children. The 2010 Census found that the number of single-parent households headed by the father increased 65 percent since the 2000 census. The research was based on a national HHS survey of 110,000 households conducted last year. Programs to cover children in low-income families include Medicaid, which

covers 30 million people in low-income families. Medicaid currently covers one in five children in the United States. The HHS research was part of a study to gather more detailed information about children with and without health insurance. Previous research had shown that about 9.2 million children, or 12.1 percent of all children lacked health coverage. The new research found that 15.4 percent of all children, or 9.6 million children, lacked health care coverage.

3. A bizarre situation finally came to a conclusion Wednesday. Minnie Cosby, 43, of 487 Jamestown Drive, is happy the episode is concluded. She wants to get on with her life. Local police are happy, too. Cosby was constantly calling police. In fact, she had called them 163 times over the past six months. The calls to police were complaints about vandalism, crank calls or prowlers. Cosby also complained that someone was stalking her. Police could never find any evidence to arrest anyone in any of the alleged crimes. Cosby told police someone had turned her gas outdoor grill on several times and left items burning on the cooking surface. Graffiti had been spray painted on the aluminum siding of her home and on her driveway several times over the six-month period. The driveway also had been strewn with broken glass, nails and screws on several occasions. On several other occasions, litter and garbage had been strewn about Cosbys yard. In another complaint, Cosby told police someone had sliced a 50-foot garden hose to pieces. Several times, Cosby complained to police that someone tampered with her car and she had to make mechanical repairs to the vehicle. Cosby also complained of numerous crank and harassing calls. Cosby complained about the calls to the telephone company, which put a trace on her telephone line. However, the calls were always made from pay telephones around the city. Cosby told police she thought the vandalism was being done by her neighbor or her neighbor's children. She told police that she has had strained relations with her neighbor for several years. Police staked out Cosbys house on several occasions, but were unable to catch anyone. "This has been a case that has stumped the department for a long time. We spent a lot of time and effort trying to track down leads but didn't have a lot of success," said police Chief Barry Koperud. Police didn't have success until Monday night when patrol officers caught a man prowling around Cosbys house. The man was dressed in black and wore a ski mask. He had a screwdriver, a utility razor knife and a can of spray paint in his possession. The color of the spray paint matched the color that had been sprayed on Cosbys house on several occasions. When police arrested the man, he had allegedly flattened three tires on Cosbys car and was attempting to flatten the fourth tire. Police charged Randall Cosby, 47, of 5845 South Conway Road, with more than 150 counts of criminal mischief, loitering and prowling, harassment, stalking by communication, possessing instruments of crime, criminal trespass and defiant trespass. The suspect, Randall Cosby, is the ex-husband of Minnie Cosby. They have been divorced for four years. Police said that Randall Cosby was angry with his ex-wife after she had requested money from him to make repairs to the house they had once shared. Minnie Cosby said the repairs were supposed to have been made to the house as part of their divorce agreement, but Randall had refused to abide by the agreement. Cosby is a 20-year veteran of the citys police department. During that

Name _____   **Class** _____   **Date** _____

time he was awarded several commendations for public service for his work as a patrol officer. Randall Cosby responded to several of the vandalism calls and twice was on the stakeout unit watching the former Mrs. Cosbys home. "I'm just glad this is over. The police probably thought I was crazy making all those calls to them about the things that were happening to me. But I wasn't crazy. I feel sorry for Randall. This wouldn't have happened if he just would have done what he was supposed to do. Maybe some time in prison will let him cool off and think about what he's done. I hope he goes to jail because at least in jail, he won't be able to hurt me anymore," Minnie Cosby said.

4. County sheriff's deputies were in for a bit of a surprise Wednesday. Your county implemented a new program nine months ago. The program requires inmates at the county prison to perform "service" work to help pay for their incarceration. The program is part of the county probation departments pre-release program that gives county inmates an opportunity to qualify for work release and earn credit for early release from incarceration. The service work can vary, but often includes picking up litter along highways or working as laborers on county road crews trimming grass and weeds along county roads. Sheriff's deputies had a road crew picking up litter along Collins Road Wednesday afternoon at 3:10 p.m. There were 18 prisoners working on the litter collection crew and two sheriffs deputies and a corrections officer guarding them. Marvin Kehole, 28, of 182 West Broadway Avenue was one of the inmates. Kehole was serving time for driving under the influence of alcohol, public drunkenness and possession of marijuana. The prison inmates were dressed in bright orange shirts and bright orange and white striped pants. Suddenly there was a loud boom and a 1998 Ford Taurus struck the back of the box van that the corrections officer was driving. The passenger box van is used to transport the inmate workers to and from the job site. Paula Andrews, 65, of 4030 New Orleans Ave., told police she reached down to adjust the volume on the cars radio. When she looked back up, the van was there and she could not get stopped. Andrews was not injured in the crash. When the sheriffs deputies checked the prison inmates after the commotion, they were missing one inmate. Keyhole had escaped. Officers called for help and 20 police and corrections officers, including a K-9 unit responded to the scene. Police and corrections officers found Keholes prison uniform behind a storage shed at a nearby house. Police called in a helicopter to aid in the search. The K-9 unit tracked the scent trail of Kehole for nearly 2 miles to the door of Jim's Lounge, located in the 4700 block of Collins Road. Police found Kehole inside, sitting at the bar drinking a beer. "He was sitting there just as cool as you please when we came into Jim's. He didn't offer any resistance when we arrested him. He had slipped away when our attention was diverted by that accident. He ran to a nearby house and stole some clothing off a clothesline, then walked down a couple of back streets to Jim's. Kehole told us he just wanted a drink. He must have been really thirsty because this is going to cost him when he gets in front of that judge," said sheriff's deputy Roger Horan. Kehole was charged with escape, theft of property and violation of prison regulations regarding consuming alcohol.

5. It was a potential tragedy that your citys police, rescue and fire officials say was just barely averted. James Shanahan, his two daughters Alyssa and Adrienne, and his wife, Mary, were traveling from Grand Rapids, Mich. They were flying near your city when the plane they were in had to make an emergency landing. James Shanahan is a licensed pilot. He has been flying for 30 years. He has never had a problem in all that time. No one was seriously injured, but James Shanahan was admitted to Mercy Hospital for observation. Mrs. Shanahan was treated for a broken wrist and a laceration on her forehead and released. Adrienne suffered minor cuts and bruises. Alyssa was not injured. The plane was a four-passenger Mooney Executive 21 propeller-driven, fixed-wing aircraft. The undercarriage of the plane sustained minor damage. There was a small fuel spill, according to the fire department. "They were very fortunate. It could have been much worse than it was. There were a lot of startled people when that plane came at them," said Fire Chief Tony Sullivan. Police Chief Barry Kopperud said the Shanahans left Grand Rapids early in the morning. The flight was proceeding normally until the plane was 100 miles east of the city. The plane began to wander off course and was contacted by the control tower at City Regional Airport. A girls voice responded to the control tower. "The girl I talked to on the radio told me the pilot was having problems. She told me he had slumped in his seat and was unconscious. I could hear the passengers screaming in the background. It was really confusing. I think they were getting a bit panicky up there," said control tower flight manager Peter Jacobs. Police said James Shanahan lost consciousness as he was about to contact the tower to request an emergency landing. His wife, Mary, told police her husband began complaining about not feeling well. He told her that he felt dizzy and couldn't get his breath. She said he suddenly slumped over in his seat and the plane went into a shallow dive. "There was nothing I could do. I was in the back passenger seat with my daughter Adrienne. I couldn't reach the controls. And even if I could have, I don't think I could have helped because I never learned how to fly. I hate flying," Mrs. Shanahan said. Kopperud said Aylssa Shanahan was seated beside her father. It was she who responded to the towers call about the plane wandering off course. Alyssa pulled her fathers arms away from the controls and his legs off the rudder pedals. She then took over the controls of the aircraft and called the tower for help to land the plane. Jacobs stayed in contact with Alyssa and gave her instructions on what to do. He talked to her the entire time and directed other aircraft away from the airport until the emergency was over. Alyssa was able to locate the airport and brought the plane down. When the plane landed, it overshot the runway and skidded across an open field. The landing gear of the plane collapsed and the plane plowed through a chain-link fence and came to a stop just 10 feet from the northbound lane of Interstate 51. The interstate was crowded with traffic at the time of the accident. The accident occurred at 4:05 p.m., police said. No one on the ground was injured. Alyssa is 12 years old, 4 feet 3 inches tall and weighs 88 pounds. "I've been flying with my Daddy since I was a little girl. He taught me all about flying and even let me handle the controls sometimes. I was a little scared because I couldn't reach the rudder pedals very well. But I couldn't be too scared because I want to be a pilot like my Daddy someday. I was more worried about my Daddy because I didn't know what happened to him. I just wanted to get on the ground and get help for him," Alyssa said. Doctors at Mercy Hospital said Mr. Shanahan was in satisfactory condition after suffering an allergic reaction to a prescription medicine he had begun taking that morning.

EXERCISE 4: The Body of a News Story

Reporting Controversial Stories
(Quoting Opposing Viewpoints)

INSTRUCTIONS: Write complete news stories about the following controversies. As you write the stories, present both sides of each controversy as fully and as fairly as possible. Also, try to integrate those conflicting viewpoints. Instead of reporting all the opinions voiced by the first source, and then all the conflicting opinions voiced by the second source, try—when appropriate—to report both opinions about the story's most important issue and then both opinions about the second, third and fourth issues.

STORY 1: SCHOOL BOARD BAN

FACTS: The school board in your town made a unanimous decision Tuesday night. It wasn't a popular decision with some students and parents. But school board members said they made the decision for the safety of athletes participating in sports in the school district. The vote was 9 to nothing. The board voted to ban boys from playing on girls' teams. The policy was implemented after four boys tried out for and made the high schools girls filed hockey team last year. The boys played on the team last fall and helped the team make the state playoffs. The policy banning boys from girls teams says the size, speed and power of male athletes poses a hazard for female players. Several schools that played your towns high school team last year forfeited their games rather than take a chance of fielding their girls against the boys on the team. The policy takes affect immediately. The policy will ban boys from playing on the girls field hockey, volleyball and softball teams

ONE SIDE: High school athletic director Hugh Baker told the board that such a blanket policy could hurt the schools athletics program because the school would have to forfeit games to other teams. "If safety is the issue of concern for the board, then our girls teams would have to forfeit games if there are boys on the opposing teams. If we can't have boys on our teams because the board is afraid girls will get hurt, then our teams can't play against teams that have boys on their teams. Our girls field hockey team would have had to forfeit at least ten of their 18 games last season because we played other schools that had boys on their teams. It would be unfair to force our field hockey team to have a losing record every year because it has to forfeit all those games. Some of the schools we play are smaller schools and they wouldn't be able to field enough players if they didn't allow boys and girls to play on the same team." Jacob Stevens is a senior at the high school. He played on the girls field hockey team last year. He was looking forward to playing on the team his senior year. He spoke to the board during the meeting. "I don't think it is fair. There are countries in the world where men's field hockey is a recognized sport. Not every guy wants to play football, basketball or baseball. Field hockey is a fast and exciting sport that requires a lot of skill. I enjoy playing the game and I haven't had any of the other female players on the team complain about my being there. If we can't play with the girls, we wouldn't be able to play. There are not enough boys interested to create a mens field hockey team."

THE OTHER SIDE: School board member Jane Tribitt voted for the policy. She proposed the ban after receiving complaints from parents in both the home district and away districts. "I just don't believe the sexes should be mixed in this case. The boys are just too big and physical and it intimidates the girls on the team. It is a matter of safety. And there are other teams that have no boys on their teams that do not want to play our school for whatever reason because there are boys on the team. I think other schools will adopt policies similar to this one and ban boys from their teams as well. The question of forfeiting games will then become a moot point." Sandra Adler is a parent whose daughter was a senior on last years team along with the four boys. Adler also was an all-state consensus pick as player of the year during her senior year on the girls field hockey team thirty years ago. Her husband is Stuard Adler, minister of the Church of Christ. "I just don't think it is healthy mentally or physically to have the boys and girls playing on the same team. There probably are girls who want to play on the boys football or baseball teams, but they are not allowed. So I don't think the boys should be allowed to take over the girls team sports. Just because there are not enough boys interested in the sport to field their own team is not justification for their being allowed to join the girls team."

STORY 2: PAINT CAN PROJECT

FACTS: It is a debate that has been raging for weeks. Your City Council voted last night on a motion to approve a controversial sale and improvement project. The vote, which was 4–3, was a close one. The meeting drew a large crowd of supporters and opponents to the proposal. The city owns an old metal water tank. The tank can hold 200,000 gallons of water. The city no longer uses the water tank because it is obsolete. It has sat empty for the past seven years. The city stopped using the tank because of state government regulations regarding open sources of water and possible contamination. The city now uses completely enclosed water storage facilities. The tank is 50 feet tall and 25 feet in diameter. More than 100 residents attended the meeting, which was held at 7:30 p.m. in City Hall. A local businessman who owns a paint manufacturing plant near the site offered to buy the water tower. He wants to clean up the tower, which is scarred by corrosion and peeling paint. He wants to repaint it so it resembles a giant can of paint and put his company logo on it. Residents in the area want the city to tear the water tower down because they claim it is an eyesore. They also claim that the tank poses an environmental hazard because lead in the peeling paint is leaching into the ground around the tank. It would cost the city 483 thousand dollars to demolish the water tank and haul it away. The paint company has offered $50,000 to buy the tank from the city.

ONE SIDE: William Krueger, 284 Erie Ave., is the president of Alladdin Paints. Kruegar said at the meeting: "This is in the best interest of the town and will be a novel way to promote my business. The city would have to spend nearly half a million dollars to tear that tank down and I'm offering to provide the city with some extra revenue instead. The promotional value of that tank painted up as a giant paint can is invaluable to my company. It also will promote the city as a business-friendly city because news organizations from all over the country will want to do stories on it. The American Paint Manufacturers Association is ready to help pay some of the cost to clean up the tank and paint it. I think it is a win-win situation for the city." Barton Masters, executive director of the Chamber of Commerce attended the meeting in support of the proposal. "This is a unique way to deal with that water tank, which has been an eyesore for years. It shows that business and government can work cooperatively to solve problems in a community. When it is renovated and painted, I'll bet money that residents in the area will be surprised at how attractive it looks."

THE OTHER SIDE: Amanda Blake, 3314 Santana Blvd., lives near the water tank. She can see the top of it from the back porch of her house. "If Mr. Masters thinks that can will look so attractive, why doesn't he put one in his backyard. Santana Boulevard residents have had to put up with a lot of neglect by city officials over the years. We have requested, begged and threatened to sue to have that tank removed. It is an eyesore and a potential environmental hazard. Tests have shown that the original paint on that tank contains lead and that lead is leaching into the ground. Kids play near that area. What is going to happen to them? Do city officials think that a new coat of paint is going to solve that problem? It may sound like a bargain to sell the problem to someone else, but selling the tank is not going to solve the real problem—how to enhance life for the residents of Santana Boulevard. The city should tear the tank down and clean up the site." Roger

Name _____ Class _____ Date _____

Ellam, 2481 Santana Blvd., opposes the idea: "Four years ago the city promised us that it would tear the tank down. And four years later it is still sitting there. I drive by that thing every day on my way to work. You don't have to drive by it because you don't live near it. The residents of Santana Boulevard deserve better from their elected officials. You're trying to save money at our expense." City council member Alice Cycler voted against the proposal: "I can't support this proposal because we promised residents that we would clean up that section of Santana Boulevard and provide funds for residential revitalization. I don't think a giant paint can will provide a symbol of neighborhood revitalization."

STORY 3: HOUSING PROJECT

FACTS: Your City Council voted last night on a proposal to locate a low-income housing project in the 4200 block of Forest Boulevard, which is part of the Creekside Village subdivision. The project would consist of 14 two-story brick buildings. Each building would house 6 to 8 families. The project would cost $6 million and would be federally subsidized. It would serve the elderly, the handicapped and low-income families. After last nights meeting, at which many people loudly and vigorously objected to the plans, the City Council vetoed the proposal by a unanimous vote of 7 to 0. The plans were presented to the City Council by the Tri-County Housing Authority, which is a semi-autonomous public body but which needs the approval of local governing boards to locate its projects within the boundaries of their jurisdictions.

ONE SIDE: The director of the City Housing Authority, Tom Chinn Onn, told the City Council before the vote: "I'm really disappointed in the opposition here tonight. We have a backlog of over 900 applicants waiting to find public housing. This would go a long way toward meeting that need. Low income people are the ones who'll be hurt, badly hurt, if this isn't approved. Everyone seems to be saying they want to help the poor, but no one wants them in their own neighborhoods. Everyone complains when we try to place them in a nice neighborhood. And a lot of what you're hearing tonight about this project is emotional rather than factual. Its all scare tactics. Studies done by Don Brame (the citys traffic operations engineer) show that the project would add only 600 to 800 additional vehicles on the areas roads on a daily basis, and thats a very liberal estimate considering that about a third of the units would be occupied by older people who probably wouldn't drive much. The elderly also wouldn't need other city facilities, like schools. Now, we've already spent more than $160,000 planning this project, and all the money will be wasted, just totally wasted, if you reject this proposal, and we've got nowhere else to go with it. Everyone says they want to help the poor, but they want to help them somewhere else. Thats real hypocrisy. This is a chance for the members of this council to be real statesmen and do some real good for some needy people. This means a lot to them, so I ask you to approve these plans."

THE OTHER SIDE: Residents of the neighborhood voiced the following complaints during the council meeting. Frank D. Shadgett of 8472 Chestnut Drive said, "This thing would cause all sorts of problems: crowded roads, crowded schools, more kids in the streets. We don't have enough parks, and there's only one junior high school and one high school that serve our neighborhood, and both have been filled for years. Now, if you dump this project on us, you'll have to bus some of our children out of their neighborhood schools, or you'll have to bring in some portable classrooms. There are other places that could handle the project better. It just doesn't fit in our neighborhood. You should come out and look at the area before coming up with an idea like this. A lot of our homes cost $185,000 or $230,000 or more. You put this project in the middle of them, and it'll hurt our property values." Another person, James Lasater of 374 Walnut Drive said: "The area is zoned for single-family homes and thats why we invested here. We've got our life savings in our homes, and this will hurt us. We've got no lack of compassion for the cause, but it just doesn't belong here. We want to protect our neighborhood and keep our neighborhood the way it is. We object to this bunch of bureaucrats coming in and changing its character. Its a good area to live in, and we don't want that to change." An attorney representing the neighborhood, Michael Perakis, said: "The area is one of the most stable and beautiful single-family neighborhoods in the city, and these people are only interested in maintaining that status. Right now, you're in danger of violating your own laws if you put this project in Creekside Village. There's been no proper hearings to rezone the land, and this project doesn't fit its current zoning restrictions. The zoning laws are intended to prevent this very kind of thing, this invasion of a residential neighborhood with a nonconforming project of any type."

STORY 4: BANNING FREE SPEECH

FACTS: There was a protest in your city over a new law passed by city officials that bans smoking in all public places. The new ordinance passed by City Council late last year even banned smoking in restaurants and bars. The ordinance was passed over the objections of restaurant and tavern owners and a group called Stop Making Ordinances; Keep Every Right Safe, or SMOKERS. Last week a group of SMOKERS led a protest against the law. The eight men and five women walked into the Steak & Ale Restaurant and chained themselves to the bar. They then lit cigarettes and cigars and began smoking them. The restaurant's manager called police, who had to use bolt cutters to free the protesters from the bar and then carry each of the protesters out of the bar to waiting patrol cars. City officials figure it cost several thousand dollars to arrest and process the 13 protesters. The city is now considering another ordinance. This one would require protesters who get arrested to pay the cost of the time and effort it takes police to place them in custody. City officials say it costs the city too much money to arrest and process the protesters. To offset the cost, protesters who get arrested would have to pay a $300 processing fee in addition to any fines or court costs for charges filed against them. City council member William Belmonte proposed the ordinance and made a motion to have city attorney Allen Farci explore the legal aspects of such an ordinance. Belmonte wants the city to vote on the proposed ordinance next month. City council approved Belmonte's motion to explore the need for and legality of such an ordinance by a vote of 5–2.

ONE SIDE: In interviews this morning after Tuesday night's meeting, city council member William Belmonte said: "This is not about taking away the people's right to protest. It is a matter of trying to stretch scarce city resources. I support the people's right to free speech, but I don't support their right to be arrested for free. Someone has to bear the cost of securing public safety and it shouldn't always be the public. These people who protest are trying to disrupt our community and make a spectacle of themselves. They're like spoiled children who can't get their way so they want to scream and shout about it. They think if they disrupt our city and our lives and hurt us economically, we'll cave in to their demands. Well I've got news for them, this city is not going to be held hostage by a bunch of hooligans." In a second interview with city attorney Allen Farci, Farci said: "I think the city is on solid legal ground here. I think the state and federal courts would allow us to add a fee to someone being arrested as a protester. We impose fees on criminals all the time to generate revenue to support the courts, and I see this as no different. We are not stopping people from protesting. They can still protest in a peaceful manner. It is when people break the law and try to get themselves arrested in order to tie up law enforcement and disrupt life in the city that it becomes a problem financially for the city."

THE OTHER SIDE: In a follow-up interview later that day, Lydia Hanson, 880 6th St., a lawyer and member of your states Civil Liberties Union, said: "We don't live in a dictatorship. Protesting government policies and actions is as American as apple pie. This is a tactic that totalitarian regimes use to control their people. They make the people pay for the cost of prosecution so people are afraid to protest onerous government policies. If the city council is going to treat SMOKERS like this, are they going to treat all protesters the same. What about those who demonstrate about issues the city council supports?

Name _____   **Class** _____   **Date** _____

Are they going to have them arrested and make them pay the processing fee? I think this crazy idea by city council should be challenged all the way to the Supreme Court." Alan Macco, 503 29th St., a musician whose band plays many of the bars in the city, had this to say: "Belmonte is a former smoker and he is the one who proposed the original no smoking ban that prompted all this. Now he even wants to take away the ability of people to speak out. He won't admit he was wrong about the no smoking ban; he just wants to silence those who don't agree with him." In a telephone interview, Beverly Cheng, executive director of the State Restaurant Association, said: "This is an example of government taking a good thing too far and then compounding the problem. I see nothing wrong with having separate areas in a restaurant or bar for smokers and non-smokers. That is fair to everyone. But to ban a whole segment of society from doing something they enjoy is unfair. And then to persecute them even more by taking away their right to voice their opinion is adding insult to injury."

Name _____   Class _____   Date _____

EXERCISES TO ACCOMPANY CHAPTER **10**

Quotations and Attribution

EXERCISE 1: Improving Quotations and Attribution

SECTION I: PARAPHRASING WEAK QUOTATIONS

INSTRUCTIONS: Rewrite the following quotations more simply as paraphrases.

1. "To tell you the truth, I would, uh, I'd be disinclined to recommend buying any shares of General Motors at this, uh, present moment in time," the financial planner said.

2. "I want to tell you that, like, uh, you know man, what we're aiming for is to get everybody to realize that, uh, suicide is never an acceptable option for anyone under any circumstances, not even like, uh, the terminally ill," she said.

3. "My brother was driving down this road and, uh, at first I didn't know what happened. Like I wasn't watching the road or nothing and didn't know what the hell it was. Then, uh, so I looked out the back window and saw this kid lying all bloody and dead on the road. Then I knew what we'd hit," he said.

SECTION II: AVOIDING DOUBLE ATTRIBUTION

INSTRUCTIONS: Rewrite the following sentences, attributing them only once.

1. A report issued Tuesday by the U.S. Department of Justice said the number of serious crimes committed in the U.S. declined 3% last year.

2. Speaking to more than 3,000 people in the Municipal Auditorium, she continued by stating that only the Democratic Party favors universal health care.

3. The Census Bureau issued a report today stating that, according to data it gathered last year, 5.2 million people in the U.S. are homeless, including 620,000 children.

SECTION III: CORRECTING PLACEMENT ERRORS

INSTRUCTIONS: Correct the placement of the attribution in the following sentences.

1. People under 18, she said, should not be allowed to drive.

2. Another important step is to, she said, lower the books' prices.

3. "The average shoplifters are teen-age girls who steal for the thrill of it, and housewives who steal items they can use. They don't have to steal; most have plenty of money, but they don't think it's a crime. They also think they'll get away with it forever," Valderrama said.

Name _____ Class _____ Date _____

SECTION IV: CONDENSING WORDY ATTRIBUTION

INSTRUCTIONS: The attributions in the following sentences are too wordy. They appear in italics and contain a total of 76 words. How many of the words can you eliminate? Rewrite the attribution, if necessary.

1. *She concluded her speech by telling the scouts that* the jamboree will be held from August 7–13.

2. *He was quick to point out the fact that, in his opinion,* the president has "failed to act effectively to reduce the federal deficit."

3. *She expressed her feelings by explaining that she believes that* anyone convicted of drunken driving should lose their license for life.

4. *She also went on to point out the fact that the results of federal studies show that,* by recycling 1 ton of paper, you can save 17 trees.

5. *In a speech to the students Tuesday, he first began by offering them his opinion that* their professors should emphasize teaching, not research.

6. *He continued by urging his listeners to remember the critical point that* the country's energy policy has failed: that the United States is not developing alternative fuels, nor preserving existing fuels.

SECTION V: IMPROVING QUOTATIONS

INSTRUCTIONS: Correct all errors of punctuation and wording and placement of attribution in the following quotations.

1. He said: "after a certain number of years, our faces become our biographies".

2. Andy Rooney declared "if dogs could talk, it would take a lot of fun out of owning one".

3. "Because that's where the money is" Willie Sutton answered when asked why he robbed banks.

4. He continued by claiming that there are "two" types of people who complain about their taxes: "men" and "women."

5. "Blessed is he" said W.C. Bennett "who expects no gratitude, for he shall not be disappointed." explained Bennett.

6. Mother Teresa then spoke to the youths, telling them that "The most terrible poverty is loneliness and the feeling of being unwanted."

7. Andy Rooney was also the individual who once announced that: "For those who don't get killed or wounded, war is a great experience."

8. He went on to also state that, getting older is doing "less and less" for the first time and "more and more" for the last time.

9. "My views on birth control" said Robert F. Kennedy "Are somewhat distorted by the fact that I was the seventh of nine children".

10. Being a police officer is not always fun and exciting, says Hennigan. "Some things you'd just as soon forget." "Some things you do forget."

11. "The art of taxation." claimed a French statesman long ago "Consists in so plucking the goose as to obtain the most feathers with the least hissing".

12. When asked why she wants to do it, she said she "loves it. My friends think I'm a little crazy, but this is what I want to do with my life—be a highway patrolman."

13. Howe, a junior majoring in nursing, announced that he dislikes the tests. "You have to study differently for multiple choice tests. You have to memorize instead of learn."

14. Dr. Hector Rivera said they diagnose for AIDS at the clinic "but do not treat the disease." "People come in to be tested scared to death." "Some leave the clinic relieved, and some don't." he said.

15. Her friendships, home, and family are the most important things in her life. "My husband is my best friend." "Maybe that's why we've lasted so long." "You really need to be friends before you're lovers".

16. "I cheat because professors give too much work." It's crazy, he said. "They don't take into consideration that some people have jobs, families and other outside interests." continued the history major.
   He then continued by adding that he's never been caught.

17. "My son thinks I'm old." "But I'm actually in good health for my age." "Of course, I have the usual aches and pains of an 80-year-old." "But I can still take care of my own house, and I still enjoy it." "My son thinks I should move into one of those retirement apartments and watch Wheel of Fortune all day." said he.

18. Jo Ann Nyez, a secretary, grew up in Milwaukee and described a childhood fear: There was this house at the end of my street and none of us would dare go near it on Halloween. It was supposed to be haunted. The story was that the wife had hung herself in the basement and the husband killed and ate rattlesnakes.

EXERCISE 2: **Wording, Placement and Punctuation**

INSTRUCTIONS: Make any changes necessary to improve the attribution in the following sentences and paragraphs. Also correct style, spelling and punctuation errors.

1. "Our goal is peace". claimed the president.

2. Benjamin Franklin said: "death takes no bribes".

Name _____ Class _____ Date _____

3. She said her son refers to her literary endeavors as, "moms writing thing".

4. He is a scuba diver and pilot. He also enjoys skydiving. "I like challenge, something exciting."

5. "The dangers promise to be of indefinite duration." the president said referring to the Mideast crisis.

6. "A free press can of course be good or bad, but, most certainly, without freedom it will never be anything but bad. . . ." "Freedom is nothing else but a chance to be better, whereas enslavement is a certainty of the worse." said the writer Albert Camus in one of his books.

7. Jesse Owens expressed the opinion that "I think that America has become too athletic." "From Little League to the pro leagues, sports are no longer recreation." "They are big business, and they're drudgery." he continued.

8. The man smiled, "It's a great deal for me." "I expect to double my money," he explained.

9. When asked what she likes most about her job as a newspaper reporter, the woman responded by saying—"I'm not paid much, but the work is important. And it's varied and exciting." She grinned: "Also, I like seeing my byline in the paper."

10. The librarian announced to reporters that the new building "will cost somewhere in the neighborhood of about $4.6 million."

11. "Thousands of the poor in the United States," said the professor, "die every year of diseases we can easily cure." "It's a crime," he said, "but no one ever is punished for their deaths."

12. Thomas said students should never be spanked. "A young boy or girl who gets spanked in front of peers becomes embarrassed and the object of ridicule."

13. The lawyer said, "He ripped the life-sustaining respirator tubes from his throat three times in an effort to die. He is simply a man" the lawyer continued "who rejects medical treatment regardless of the consequences. He wants to die and has a constitutional right to do so."

14. Bobby Knight, the basketball coach at Texas Tech University, said. "Everyone has the will to win." "Few have the will to prepare." Knight added that. "It is the preparation that counts."

15. She said she firmly believes that the federal government "must do more" to help cities "support and retrain" the chronically unemployed.

EXERCISE 3: Verbs of Attribution

INSTRUCTIONS: Below are several verbs that reporters often use as substitutes for "said" when attributing statements. Define each of these verbs and give an example of how it may be correctly used for attribution.

Name _____   Class _____   Date _____

add	mention
affirm	note
announce	observe
assert	point out
assure	pronounce
aver	propound
claim	recite
comment	respond
conclude	reveal
continue	set forth
declaim	specify
declare	state
discourse	suggest
emphasize	tell
explain	urge
express	utter
inform	warn
maintain	wonder

EXERCISE 4: Using Quotes in News Stories

INSTRUCTIONS: Write complete news stories based on the following information. Use direct quotations in each story to emphasize the highlights, but do not use quotations to tell the entire story. Use the most interesting, important and revealing quotations and paraphrase the rest of the quoted information. Correct any errors in grammar, punctuation and Associated Press style.

1. Jonathan Ashton is a congressman representing your state. He is very unhappy about a decision the House of Representatives made on a bill that was recently brought up for a vote: "The President lost a battle in Congress today. Congress decided against spending $12 million for a cause the president favored. The project involved huge dish-shaped antennas which listened for radio signals from outer space. It was cut from NASA's budget. The House today approved a $14.29 billion budget for NASA in a 355–48 vote. If the Senate agrees with the House, the space agency budget for next fiscal year will be $2 billion above current spending levels but $800 million below what the president requested. The president wanted included in the budget $12 million for the alien-search project. NASA's search for extraterrestrial intelligence, a project known as SETI, was to cost $100 million over 10 years. Its sophisticated radio antennas have picked up only static since the program began, but that does not mean that the program should be abandoned. We never may discover life beyond our own planet if we abandon the search for that life." Rep. Ronald Machtley, a Republican congressman from Rhode Island, opposes the SETI project and the money being spent

Name _____   Class _____   Date _____

on it. He had this to say: "I suggest that the money be spent on education. I'd rather see a search for terrestrial intelligence in our schools than a search for intelligent life in space that may not exist."

2. The Department of Veterans Affairs today admitted that its made a little mistake. This is what Geraldine Anderson, public affairs officer for the Department of Veterans Affairs had to say: "The mistake cost an estimated $5.7 million a year for the past eleven years. Each year, the Veterans Affairs Department pays more than $14.7 billion in disability compensation and pension benefits to more than 2.8 million veterans and to nearly 1 million surviving spouses and other dependents. An audit of those payments revealed that the Department of Veterans Affairs has been paying benefits to more than 1,200 veterans who are dead. The exact total was 1,212 veterans who were reported dead. About 100 of the veterans have been dead a decade or more. Auditors said the department could have reduced the erroneous payments by matching VA benefit payment files with death information maintained by the Social Security Administration. In the past, the department relied on voluntary reporting of deaths as a basis for ending benefits. This means the department will have to develop a new and more strenuous auditing plan to determine who is eligible for benefits and when those benefits should end. Also, the Department of Veterans Affairs will seek to bring to justice those who fraudulently took money from the department that they did not truly deserve. There are many honest and deserving veterans out there who have served their country admirably, and the department wants to continue to serve them and provide the benefits they have earned. But as we all know, it only takes a few rotten apples to spoil the whole barrel. The Department of Veterans Affairs will be implementing a new program in the next several months that will provide a more accurate accounting of the veterans who are receiving benefits and what they are receiving. We are hoping that this new effort will save the department money so there are more funds for those veterans who need our programs."

3. Dr. Cathleen Graham, M.D., is head of your citys Department of Health. At a press conference today, she announced that a prominent doctor recently revealed that he has developed AIDS. Following is what she had to say: "Todd Lefforge is an orthodontist who has been working in our community for 11 years. He is 36 years old and lives at 537 Peterson Place. He has a practice of about 750 current patients. He has treated approximately 5,000 more in the past. Three days ago he announced that he has AIDS. He was diagnosed with AIDS six days ago. He immediately closed his practice. He also wrote a letter to all his patients, mostly children, and their parents. His letter, which parents began to receive today, says, "I am very sorry for any anxiety this may cause to anyone." 'I have always followed the CDC [Centers for Disease Control] guidelines regarding infection and sterilization procedures,' he wrote. 'I feel no patients could have been infected by me.' The Department of Health has set up an emergency center at its downtown office where, starting today, his patients can be tested for the AIDS virus and counseled about their fears. In the departments conversations with Dr. Leforge, who decided to immediately close his practice, he said

he tried to be reassuring in his letter. I and the department agree that the risk is minimal. But the long odds don't lessen the fears of a parent. Since we're dealing primarily with children, its more emotional. Its going to be a traumatic time for them. The testing which will be done in Room 103 of the Patterson Health Center Building on State Street is free. The only thing any former patient of Dr. Lefforge will need is a form of identification. Dr. Leforge has already turned over the names of his patients to the Health Department."

EXERCISES TO ACCOMPANY CHAPTER (11)

Interviewing

EXERCISE 1: Discussion Questions

1. How would you respond to a source who, several days before a scheduled interview, asked for a list of the questions you intended to ask?

2. How would you respond to a source who insisted on approving before publication all direct and indirect quotations you planned to attribute to her?

3. Do you agree that reporters have an obligation to inform their sources when they plan to record an interview even when it's legal to do so?

4. If a story's publication is likely to embarrass a source, do reporters have a responsibility to warn the source of that possibility? Does it matter whether the source is used to dealing with reporters?

5. What should you do if a person you interview alleges that another person engaged in sexual misconduct? What steps should you, could you, take to verify the information? Does your decision about how to handle the information vary with whether the person accused of sexual misconduct is a public figure, such as a celebrity or a politician, instead of a private individual?

6. Would you be willing to interview a mother whose son just died? Would it matter whether her son drowned in a swimming pool, was slain, or was a convicted killer executed in a state prison?

7. Imagine that you wrote a front-page story about students' use of marijuana on your campus. To obtain the story, you promised several sources that you would never reveal their identities. If, during a subsequent legal proceeding, a judge ordered you to identify your sources, would you do so? Or would you be willing to go to jail to protect your sources?

EXERCISE 2: Interviews

Interview With an Injured Bicyclist

INSTRUCTIONS: Write a news story based on the following interview with Marsha L. Taylor, conducted this morning, two days after she was released from a hospital after being injured in a bicycling accident. "Q" stands for the questions that Taylor was asked during the interview at her home, and "A" stands for her

Name _____   **Class** _____   **Date** _____

answers, which may be quoted directly. Taylor manages a McDonald's restaurant and lives at 2012 Lincoln Boulevard in your city.

Q: How long have you been bicycling?

A: I started when I was in college, but I didn't do any serious cycling until after I had graduated. I spent that first summer looking for work, and cycling was a way of filling in time and keeping fit while I waited for interviews. Eventually I got involved with some groups of cyclists and participating in weekend rides and even some races. Since then it's been a major part of my life. I can't imagine what my life would be like without bicycling.

Q: How active have you been in bicycling recently?

A: I rode a lot this year. Um, I guess I must have ridden at least maybe 3,500 miles because in the spring I rode in the annual Governors Bicycle Tour, which goes across the state. And in the fall I rode in a tour across the United States.

Q: How did your accident happen?

A: Well, a lot of it is hazy to me, but it happened shortly after I finished the U.S. tour. I had been back in town about two weeks and I was just out for a short ride of an hour or so. I was riding down 72nd Street almost to Southland Boulevard when a car hit me from behind and sent me flying off my bike. That's all I remember until I was in the hospital.

Q: What were your injuries?

A: Gee, you might as well ask what wasn't injured. I had a mild concussion, a broken neck, six broken ribs, a broken arm, and a broken pelvis.

Q: Were the doctors worried about your condition?

A: Yeah, somewhat. They didn't think there was anything they couldn't control, but there was a lot of stuff broken. They were especially concerned about the broken neck. One doctor said I had what they call a hangman's fracture. She said it was a miracle that I wasn't paralyzed.

Q: Was your recovery pretty smooth?

A: No. In fact I got worse at first. After a couple of weeks, they sent me to a rehabilitation facility, but then I developed complications. The doctors discovered I had some internal injuries. My intestine was perforated, and my liver and gall bladder were injured. All that caused my skin to change color, start turning bright orange. When my mother saw me, she said I looked like a Halloween pumpkin. I had to go back to the hospital because of those complications. But for that, I probably would have been out in two months instead of four. I still have to go back for rehabilitation three times a week.

Q: Have you changed your attitude about cycling since your accident?

A: No. I still want to ride. If I could, I'd be out there right now, but it's hard to ride a bike when you have to use crutches. If you, you know, take precautions and are careful, bicycling's pretty safe.

Q: What kind of precautions?

A: Well, the main thing, you know, is protective clothing, especially the helmet. I never ride unless I have my helmet. It probably saved my life this time.

Q: How long have you lived here?

A: Let's see, ah 15, years now, ever since I started work for McDonald's.

Q: How long have you been manager there?

A: Four years.

Q: How old are you?

A: Ah, 37. Old enough, yeah.

EXERCISE 3: Interviews

Interview with a Robbery Victim

INSTRUCTIONS: Write a news story based on the following interview with Michele Schipper, a sophomore majoring in journalism at your college. The interview provides a verbatim account of a robbery that occurred yesterday. "Q" stands for the questions Schipper was asked during an interview this morning, and "A" stands for her answers, which may be quoted directly. (This is a true story, told by a college student.)

Q: Could you describe the robbery?

A: I pulled up into the parking lot of a convenience store on Bonneville Drive, but I pulled up on the side and not in front where I should have, and I was getting out of my car, and I was reaching into my car to pull out my purse when this guy, 6 foot tall or whatever, approached me and said, "Give me your purse." I said, "OK." I barely saw him out of the corner of my eye. And then, I, um, so I reached in to get my purse. And I could see him approaching a little closer. Before then, he was 4 or 5 feet away. So I turned around and kicked him in the groin area, and he started going down, but I was afraid he wouldn't stay down, that he would seek some kind of retribution. So when he was down, I gave him a roundhouse to the nose. I just hit him as hard as I could, an undercut as hard as I could. And I could hear some crunching, and some blood spurted, and he went on the ground, and I got in my car, and I went away. I called the cops from a motel down the street. They asked where he was last I seen him, and I said. "On the ground."

Q: Did the police find him?

A: No, he was gone.

Q: Had you taken judo or some type of self-defense course?

A: No, but I used to be a tomboy and I used to wrestle with the guys, my good friends, when I was young. It was a good punch. I don't know, I was just very mad. My dad, he works out with boxing and weightlifting and everything, and I've played with that, so I've got the power.

Name _____   Class _____   Date _____

Q: Could you describe the man?

A: I didn't see him well enough to identify him, really, but I hope he thinks twice next time.

Q: What time did the robbery occur?

A: This was about 4 in the afternoon, broad daylight, but there were no other cars parked around, though.

Q: Did you see the man when you drove up, or was he hiding?

A: There was a dumpster, and I guess he came from behind the dumpster, like he was waiting there, just like he was waiting there. And I guess he was waiting around the dumpster, because no one was standing around when I pulled up, I remember that.

Q: Were there any witnesses who could describe the man?

A: There was no one around, there were no cars parked. The clerks were inside the store. I didn't see any pedestrians around and, after I did it, I didn't wait to find if there were any witnesses because I wanted to leave right away.

Q: Was the man armed?

A: Out of the corner of my eye I realized I didn't see any weapon. And I guess I thought he was alone. You register some things; you just don't consciously realize it.

Q: What was your first reaction, what did you think when he first approached and demanded your purse?

A: I didn't think of anything, really, you know. I just reacted. I was very, really indignant. Why, you know, just because he wanted my purse, why should he have it? There was really only $10 in there, and I probably wouldn't really do it again in the same situation. And my parents don't know about it because they would be very angry that I fought back.

Q: Had you ever thought about being robbed and about what you would do, about how you would respond?

A: It just came instinctively, and after the incident, you know, I was shaking for about an hour afterwards.

Q: About how long did the robbery last?

A: It really only lasted a second, just as long as it would take for you to kick someone and then to hit them and then drive away in the car. It really only lasted a second.

EXERCISE 4: Interviews

Sleep Shortage

INSTRUCTIONS: Write a news story based on the following interview with Diana Gant, a member of the psychology faculty at your institution. Gant is recognized as one of the nation's leaders in the study of sleep. The interview provides a verbatim account of an interview you conducted today in her office. "Q" stands for the questions that you asked Gant, and "A" stands for her answers, which may be quoted directly.

Q: You're a professor in the Psychology Department?

A: That's right, for 17 years now. That's how long I've been here, ever since I finished graduate school.

Q: Have you been studying sleep all that time?

A: Even earlier. I started when I was a graduate student and wrote my thesis, then my dissertation, about sleep.

Q: How much sleep have you found most people need a night?

A: Most people need 9 to 10 hours a night to perform optimally. Some should be taken in afternoon naps.

Q: I read somewhere that most people need only 7 or 8 hours of sleep a night and that there are people who need only 4 or 5.

A: Nine hours is better. I know not everyone agrees with me, but that's what I keep finding. Think of sleep like exercise. People exercise because its healthy. Sleep is healthy.

Q: How much sleep does the average person actually get?

A: About 7 hours.

Q: If most people need more sleep, why aren't they getting it?

A: Believe it or not, some people think that going without sleep is the big, sophisticated, macho thing to do. They figure they don't need it, that the rules don't apply to them, that they can get more done. It may work for them for a while, but sooner or later they begin to suffer the consequences. Then you can have some real problems.

Q: How can the average person tell if he's getting enough sleep?

A: It's easy. Ask yourself: Do you usually feel sleepy or doze off when you are sitting quietly after a large lunch?

Q: What else happens if people don't get enough sleep?

A: Going without enough sleep is as much of a public and personal safety hazard as going to work drunk. It can make people clumsy, stupid, unhappy.

Q: Can you give some examples of the problem?

A: I look at a lot of disasters, really major disasters like the space shuttle Challenger, the accident at Russias Chernobyl nuclear reactor, and the Exxon Valdez oil spill. The element of sleeplessness was involved in all of them, at least contributed to all of them, and maybe—probably—caused all of them. The press focused on the possibility that the captain of the Exxon Valdez was drunk, but undershifting and long shifts on the ship may have led to the third mate's falling asleep at the wheel.

Q: How did you get interested in sleep?

A: When I started, I wanted to write about people who got little sleep and remained productive. The problem was, when my subjects arrived in laboratories and got a chance to sleep in dark, quiet rooms, they all slept for about 9 hours. That and other work convinced me that most people suffer from sleep deprivation.

Q: How do you gather your data?

A: Partly laboratory studies and partly statistics, statistics on the connection between sleeplessness and accidents. One thing I've done is study the number of traffic accidents in the state right after the shift to daylight savings time in the spring, when most people lose an hour's sleep. There's an 8% increase in accidents the day after the time change, and there's a corresponding decrease in accidents in the fall when people gain an extra hour of sleep.

Q: Why's that?

A: What we're looking at when people get up just an hour early is the equivalent of a national jet lag. The effect can last a week. It isn't simply due to loss of sleep, but complications from resetting the biological clock.

Q: How else can a lack of sleep hurt people?

A: You feel as if your clothes weigh a few extra pounds. Even more than usual, you tend to be drowsy after lunch. If, say, you cut back from 8 to 6 hours, you'll probably become depressed. Cut back even further, to 5 hours, and you may find yourself falling asleep at stoplights while driving home.

Q: If people aren't getting enough sleep, or good sleep, how can they solve the problem? What do you recommend?

A: That's easy. Almost everyone in the field agrees on that. First, you need someplace that's dark and quiet. Shut off all the lights and draw the shades. Second, its good to relax for an hour or so before going to bed. Watch TV, read a good book. Don't drink or eat a lot. That'll disturb your sleep, especially alcohol and caffeine. Plus, it should be cool, about 65 is best for good sleep. Tobacco, coffee and alcohol are all bad. As their effects wear off, your brain actually becomes more alert. Even if you fall asleep, you may find yourself waking up at 2 or 3 a.m., and then you can't get back to sleep. Also avoid chocolate and other foods that contain a lot of sugar. Finally, get a comfortable bed, and keep your bed linens clean and fresh.

EXERCISE 5: Interviews

Interview after a Murder

INSTRUCTIONS: Write a news story based on the following interview with a bookkeeper at the North Point Inn. "Q" stands for the questions she was asked during an interview at her home this morning, and "A" stands for her answers, which may be quoted directly. (The interview is based on an actual case: a robbery and murder at an elegant restaurant.)

Q: Could you start by spelling your name for me?

A: N-i-n-a C-o-r-t-e-z.

Q: You work as a bookkeeper at the North Point Inn?

A: Yes, I've been there seven years.

Q: Would you describe the robbery there yesterday?

A: It was about 9 in the morning, around 7 or 8 minutes before 9.

Q: Is that the time you usually get there?

A: At 9 o'clock, yes.

Q: How did you get in?

A: I've got a key to the employee entrance in the back.

Q: Was anyone else there?

A: Kevin Blohm, one of the cooks. He usually starts at 8. We open for lunch at 11:30, and he's in charge.

Q: Did you talk to him?

A: He came into my office, and we chatted about what happened in the restaurant the night before, and I asked him to make me some coffee. After he brought me a cup, I walked out to the corridor with him. That was the last I saw him.

Q: What did you do next?

A: I was just beginning to go through the receipts and cash from the previous night. I always start by counting the previous day's revenue. I took everything out of a safe, the cash and receipts, and began to count them on my desk.

Q: About how much did you have?

A: $6,000 counting everything, the cash and receipts from credit cards.

Q: Is that when you were robbed?

A: A minute or two or less, a man came around the corner, carrying a knife.

Q: What did you do?

A: I started screaming and kicking. My chair was on rollers, and when I started kicking, it fell. I fell on the floor, and he reached across my desk and grabbed $130 in $5 bills.

Q: Did he say anything?

A: No, he just took the money and walked out.

Q: Was he alone?

A: I don't think so. I heard someone—a man—say, "Get that money out of there." Then someone tried to open the door to my office, but I'd locked it. Three or four minutes later, the police were there.

Q: Is that when you found Mr. Blohm?

A: I went into the hallway with the police and saw blood on a door in the reception area. It was awful. There was blood on the walls and floor. Kevin was lying on the floor, dead. He had a large knife wound in his chest and another on one hand.

Q: Can you describe the man who robbed you?

A: He was about 5 feet 10, maybe 6 feet tall, in his early 20s, medium build.

Q: What was he wearing?

A: Blue jeans, a blue plaid button-up shirt and blue tennis shoes.

Q: Did you see his face?

A: He had a scarf, a floral scarf, tied around the lower part of his face, cowboy style. It covered the bottom half of his face.

Q: Did the man look at all familiar, like anyone you may have known or seen in the restaurant?

A: No.

Q: Did you notice anything unusual that day?

A: I saw a car in the parking lot when I came in, one I didn't recognize. It didn't belong to anyone who worked there, but that's all I remember.

Q: Do you have any idea why someone stabbed Blohm?

A: No. Kevin might have gotten in his way or tried to stop him or recognized him or something. I don't know. I didn't see it. I don't know anything else.

EXERCISE 6: Interviews

Hospital Bill

INSTRUCTIONS: Write a news story based on the following interview with Carmen Foucault, 1425 Penham Ave., the mother of a 23-year-old son, James, who died last week. The interview provides a verbatim account of an interview you conducted today in the family's home. "Q" stands for the questions you asked Foucault, and "A" stands for her answers, which may be quoted directly.

Q: Can you tell me what happened, why you're so upset?

A: You're damn right I will. I'm mad, mad as hell, and I want everyone to know it, to know about that damn hospital.

Q: Which hospital?

A: Mercy Hospital.

Q: When you called, you said your son died last week. Can you tell me what happened?

A: Its hard, so hard, for me to talk about it now. Its not just the sorrow, its the anger that makes it hard. I tried to do the right thing, they told me it was the right thing, and I thought my son would want it.

Name _____   **Class** _____   **Date** _____

Q: What happened to your son?

A: I worried about him. It was that Harley of his. I loved him but hated that Harley, told him he'd kill himself on it some day. Then two officers came ringing the bell last Wednesday, saying a car hit him and I'd better ride to the hospital with them.

Q: What did the doctors at Mercy Hospital tell you?

A: That I should agree to let them keep Jimmy alive long enough to donate his organs, that even though he was dying, just barely alive then, he could help save other lives.

Q: What happened then?

A: He died. We knew he was dying, maybe he was dead, I don't know. That wasn't what upset me so bad, its what happened next.

Q: Did he ever regain consciousness after the accident?

A: I don't know, I'm not sure. A nurse told me there was a flicker of brain activity, the nurse said, and they were keeping him alive. I really didn't understand that, if he was dead, why they'd do that. Then they started asking me if I would consider donating his organs. I knew its what he would want. He was always helping other people, so I agreed. I stayed there, at the hospital, until about noon Thursday. That's when they said he was gone, that they'd gotten everything they'd wanted and turned off the machines, let him die. A nurse told me it was over, that I should go home.

Q: Did the doctors tell you why they couldn't help him?

A: They said he was brain dead, that he had real serious head injuries and would never regain consciousness.

Q: What happened next?

A: They had him all cut apart, just butchered him. They didn't say it was going to be like that. Then they didn't thank me or anything. Can you believe it? My son dies, they take his parts, and then they send me a bill.

Q: A bill for what?

A: For keeping him alive an extra day, $41,000 for keeping him alive an extra day while they took his organs.

Q: Had they told you that you'd have to pay that much, or anything, to help keep him alive?

A: No, no one said anything about it, not ever.

Q: So you weren't told anything about the cost?

A: Maybe. I don't think so. I can't remember them saying anything about it. But I wasn't understanding everything, wasn't, couldn't, listen too good. He's my only son, and all I remember was them telling me he was dead, that there wasn't anything they could do for him.

Q: What's happened since then?

A: They've put a lien on his estate.

Q: A lien?

A: Oh yeah, that's what they said, but now their story's changing. Now they say they're re-examining my bill, like I should be grateful or something. Its bad enough dealing with my son's death without having to deal with this, too.

Q: Tell me more about the lien.

A: It was Thursday. He died, the day after his motorcycle was hit. And, uh, we had a funeral on Saturday. I made it Saturday so more of his friends could come. So then, uh, it was yesterday I got a notice, a registered letter, that those thieves put a lien on my son's estate for $41,000. Today, in the mail, I got the bill for $41,000 listing all the stuff the hospital did to keep Jimmy alive. I couldn't believe it! They kept him alive to get his organs, then they send me the bill for keeping him alive.

Q: Have you been told whether your son's organs helped anyone?

A: Oh yeah, that was in another of their letters. Got it from the donor bank, not the hospital. They said his organs—his heart, kidneys, liver and pancreas—saved five lives. Plus his eyes. His eyes helped someone too.

Q: What are you doing now?

A: Got myself a good lawyer, one I saw on television saying she can help people like me. She's giving 'em hell, getting things right. They're apologizing all over the place now, since she called them, the doctors and other people at the hospital, saying it was all a mistake.

Q: Did Jimmy have enough insurance to pay for his bills?

A: Yeah, I managed to talk him into that, but I can't use it now, can't pay for the funeral for my own son, can't get a gravestone, a good stone for my son. There's still that damned lien on Jimmys estate, so I can't pay for his funeral, can't use his money, and I don't have enough of my own.

Q: Is there anything else you'd like to add?

A: I'd like to meet whoever got his organs but the donor bank says it doesn't allow that. I just want to meet them, touch their chest and see who Jimmy saved.

OTHER SOURCES

Christina Snyder, a spokeswoman for the hospital, told you early today: "The lien is standard procedure to ensure a bill is paid. I agree the bill needs to be re-examined, and the donor bank will pay most of it. But Mrs. Foucault will have to pay for her sons initial treatment, and right now I don't know what that will be. Legally, we have to file a lien within 10 days after a patient dies or is discharged. Its standard practice because 50% of the trauma patients we get don't have any insurance."

Name _____ **Class** _____ **Date** _____

Irwin Greenhouse, the hospitals chief administrator, returned another of your calls just minutes ago and said: "Its a mistake the bill went to Mrs. Foucault. We're dreadfully sorry that happened and hope to learn from our mistake. The bill should have gone to the Division of Transplantation for review. We're looking at our billing procedures to make certain this never happens again. It's embarrassing, and we've already had our attorney remove the lien, told him to make it his number one priority. Normally, Mrs. Foucault would be billed the cost of normal emergency care, but the donor bank has agreed to pick up everything in this case, everything, and we'd like to apologize to Mrs. Foucault. I called her twice today to apologize, just hung up again a minute ago, and told her what we're doing, that she should be proud of her son—he's helped save several lives—and that we're sorry for our mistake, terribly sorry."

Name _____   Class _____   Date _____

EXERCISES TO ACCOMPANY CHAPTER 12

Feature Stories

EXERCISE 1: Information for Features

INSTRUCTIONS: Write feature stories based on the following sets of information. Correct all errors.

1. DEER FARMS

Kyle White is a farmer, age 41, in your county, married to his wife Rebecca, 42, and parents together of 4 children (3 girls and 1 boy). Their farm is located a distance of approximately 7 miles south of your city.

Their farm originally covered a total of 240 acres of land but eleven years ago they bought a second farm, a retiring cousins, which covered an additional 120 acres of land, so they now farm a total of 360 acres.

Little of the land is good for crops. Its too hilly and swampy, with lots of woods. A low area along the Mequin river often floods in the spring and then remains in a flooded condition for a period of time. Six years ago, Mr. White abandoned his diary herd and hay and vegetables, and pigs, chickens, and other crops and started a new crop: deer. Why? Big bucks.

Some sleek brown bucks weigh as much as 240 pounds or more. Leaner ones (visible in a pasture you visited) weigh only about 160 or so pds. They're kept on the farm by an 8-foot fence topped by barbed wire that now encircles the entire farm area. "The heaviest ones we sell," White said.

Who to? Fine restaurants throughout the entire state. They charge their diners a premium for tender venison which has much less fat than cow or pig. Some day White also hopes to sell his deer which he butchers himself directly to gourmet sections of supermarkets. Its a national trend, he said. Nearly 700 farmers nationwide now belong to the North American Deer Farmers Assn. established in 1978 by German immigrants who established the first United States venison ranch in the 1960s on a remote patch of rugged hills and woods in upstate New York. All venison ranchers now hope to capitalize on Americans current desire to be healthy—to eat well while staying fit. All tout venison as "the meat of the future"—red meat for health-conscious calorie counters. Nutritionists say among red meats only buffalo is healthier. Some animal rights activists raise a ruckus about the human consumption of deer and some consumers shudder at the thought of eating Bambi or any of the other beautiful, graceful members of the species, but deer farmers believe they can gain converts by rattling off the real statistics to further educate consumers. A 7-ounce serving of venison steak gets only 3.2% of its 316 calories from fat. Ground beef is nearly 10% fat and a 7-ounce portion weighs in at far more calories, a whopping total of 432. "Venison has less fat—and fewer calories—than even skinned chicken," White told you. At 6'2" in height, White weighs only a thin 162 pounds and is red headed with a full red beard and red mustache. Others agree about the healthful nature of venison. The American Heart Assn. lists wild game as a good choice for your daily serving of meat, poultry, or fish. Weight Watchers also recommends venison as a lean, low-calorie alternative to fatty beef. Still, its a tough sell. Tests show farm-raised venison tastes tender and mild and the meat tends to be smooth without the grains that streak beef steak. Yet many Americans tend to associate venison with the tough, gamey, shoe-leather meat that many amateur hunters often drag back home after a kill while hunting in the fall and bagging a deer that isn't as well fed and cared for as Mr. Whites.

Name _____   Class _____   Date _____

Plus there's what the farmers call the Bambi Syndrome. Graceful, brown-eyed, white-tailed deer seem to generate more sympathy than almost any other animal but dogs and cats which, by law, many states prohibit people in the U.S. from eating although both animals are eaten—elsewhere in the world along with horse. "Most consumers don't see cows as cute and cuddly like they do a veal calf or lamb or deer," said a spokesman for the national Beef Industry Council. There are doom-and-gloom predictions about the future of beef with all the new competition from deer and other species, even ostrich, but cattle ranchers tend to brush off claims of venisons surging popularity. After all, Americans gobble up, on national average for every man, woman and child in this great country, a grand total of 63 pounds of beef each year despite relentless warnings from assorted medical authorities and nutritionists against fat and cholesterol. The average American persons diet also includes 47 lbs. of pork each and every year and almost as much chicken. By comparison, the average American now eats no venison, none whatsoever, which remains at this point in time largely a novelty, sold at a few fine restaurants—never at popular, fast-food restaurants where so many Americans eat so many of their meals, but those facts also show the markets untapped potential. White says: "Everyone has prejudices, and many involving deer are unfounded: emotional, not intellectual. People see deer on television or movies, then they don't want to eat them. Kids especially, but deer are good for kids, healthy for everyone. Its healthy, tasty, and inexpensive considering the fact its all meat, not fat."

2. SCHOLARSHIP SEARCHES

Are you thinking about going to college anytime soon? Are you already there? Are you a parent with a kid in college or about to go to college. If so, beware! Don't be swindled like the thousands of other poor innocent victims swindled every year. This story comes in part out of the U.S. capital of Washington, D.C. The Federal Trade Commission issued a warning today. The F.T.C. said there are some legitimate businesses in the field but there are also bogus scholarship search services that fast talk students and their families out of millions of dollars in cash each and every single year. Just last month the same Federal Trade Commission (FTC) in Washington filed charges against eleven companies that it claims stole a total of nearly about $10 million dollars from students located in all of the 50 states who plan to start college next year or who are already in college and from their families. The companies promised to look for money to help the swindled students and their families pay the outrageous cost of college tuition, fees, room and board, and other expenses incurred while attending a college. The numbers are astonishing, truly astonishing. The FTC estimates that each and every year as many as 300,000 students and their families fall for the swindle. They're defrauded. Fooled! Cheated! Swindled! Companies promise to find a scholarship or grant, which are free, never having to be repaid. Some promise to find a scholarship or grant for each and every one of the students using their service and to return peoples money if they don't, but then they don't find financial aid and don't return the money. The FTC said today in its new warning they may never look or they may send you a useless and totally worthless computer printout which lists dozens, even hundreds, of scholarships none of which you may be currently eligible for at all. The FTC warns, simply, that "If you have to pay money to get money it might be a scam. Be wary." Matt Adamopoulos, head of the Office of Financial Aid at your school, points out the fact that high school and college counselors provide free services. So do libraries. He recommends that people use free services exclusively.

None guarantee success. "That's impossible," Adamopoulos told you in an exclusive interview today. "We can almost always help really exceptional students, and sometimes the poor. Its those in the middle we have the toughest time with," he went on to add that. The FTC also warns people not to do stupid things like give these or other companies their credit card numbers or bank account numbers or even social security numbers, since other abuses are also committed, such as emptying a victims bank account or adding other charges to his/her credit cards. But people are desperate, overwhelmed and shocked and frightened by the high and escalating and ridiculous cost of college educations in the United States nowadays which threaten to nearly bankrupt some families, especially those with multiple kids. In desperation, and because they are unfamiliar with the process, they are in many cases easy victims for swindlers. The FTC normally seeks temporary restraining orders prohibiting companies from engaging in activities the FTC has challenged. Or, the FTC freezes the companies assets. But companies can close, move to another city or state and in a matter of a very few days open a new company with a new name that continues the same practices with the same people involved. 17-year-old Susan Carigg of your city is an example of victims of the fraud along with her parents, Susan and Craig Carigg. Young Susan is a senior at your citys Martin Luther King Jr. High School and wants to attend college next year but doesn't have a lot of money or extraordinarily high grades, just a solid 3.34 gpa. She, who wants to be a nurse and her parents paid $799 to the Scholarship Search Institute 3 days after receiving a flier in the mail from its headquarters located in the city of Phoenix. The flier promised that people are "guaranteed many times their investment back" in scholarships, grants, and other financial aid. But the Carigs haven't received anything since sending in their check. Now they can't even find the company anywhere. Postal authorities they called for help are also looking for the company, and say thousands of other gullible people who fell for the scam are doing likewise. An FTC official who asked that she not be identified admitted they almost never recover anyones money. Al Giangelli, another high school senior in your city, whose parents are divorced and who lives with his mother at 214 Lake Dr., sent $999 to a similar company, Financial Aid Finders, using money he saved working at a Burger King. "I want to go to a private school," Al told you in an exclusive interview today. "I figure that'd cost maybe $20,000 a year, probably more, and they promised to help, said they help everyone, that there's lots of money for everyone. Now I'm worse off than before. I worked hard for that money and they stole it. Its a ripoff, a damn ripoff. They're crooks is what they are."

Name _____ Class _____ Date _____

EXERCISES TO ACCOMPANY CHAPTER 13

Writing for Broadcast News

EXERCISE 1: Identifying Broadcast Style

INSTRUCTIONS: The following are correctly written broadcast leads. Explain how they differ stylistically from leads written for newspapers. Think about time, verb tense, titles, personal identification, amount of information and a conversational mode.

1. Observing the 15th anniversary of Americans with Disabilities Act, President Bush said this morning that the civil rights law had improved people's lives.

2. A five-year-old girl is credited with saving a man's life near Tulsa, Oklahoma.

3. Council member Jebb Locket wants motorized scooters to be a thing of the past.

4. Four cars were stolen last night in different incidents in the downtown area.

5. The US has begun extradition procedures against the political leader of an Islamic militant group.

6. Prosecutors want more time to build a case against a city official accused of illegal trading.

7. We are in for some really warm weather tomorrow.

8. A city police officer is clinging to her life after a shooting that killed a fellow officer.

9. Purple wreaths are disappearing from cemeteries across the county.

10. Several break-ins on campus this weekend are causing dormitory residents to lock their doors more often.

EXERCISE 2: Identifying Different Broadcast Leads

INSTRUCTIONS: The following broadcast leads and the second paragraphs are written correctly. Identify the style of each lead: hard news, soft news, throwaway or umbrella.

1. LEAD: Thanksgiving holiday traffic accidents in our state have claimed at least five lives.
   REST OF THE STORY: The victims include three Jonesville residents killed in a rollover accident in Ingham County. They're identified as 22-year-old Marie Wildflower and her passengers, 28-year-old Jesse Wildflower and his sister Margaret Quinn, who was 25 years old. Officials in Greene County say 44-year-old Jimmie Lincoln and 62-year-old Zackory Timbs died in a two-car accident. Both men are Centerville residents.

2. LEAD: There is confirmation that inflation is not a problem.

   REST OF THE STORY: A representative of the Labor Department says that the June Producer Price index dropped one-tenth of one percent. Not counting food and energy, the index was ahead a modest two-tenths of one percent. The index shows a big decline in energy costs and the largest drop in fruit prices in nearly 20 years.

3. LEAD: A New York man who tried to exterminate his girlfriend's family will spend the rest of his life in prison.

   REST OF THE STORY: A federal judge in Rochester, New York, today gave Hiram Evans five consecutive life terms and four additional life sentences to be served concurrently.

4. LEAD: Suburban Detroit automotive supplier Lear is cutting 28-hundred jobs.

   REST OF THE STORY: The cuts amount to about four percent of Lear's employees. About eleven hundred of the employees will be cut in North America, the rest in Europe. Company representative Jill Li says that Lear hopes the reorganization saves more than 40-million dollars yearly.

5. LEAD: Shakespeare's ghost may live again.

   REST OF THE STORY: After about 400 years, actors are again on the stage of the Globe Theatre in London. It's a copy of the old building where the playwright's productions were first performed.

6. LEAD: About a dozen people were killed this morning when a charter flight out of Chicago hit thunderstorms.

   REST OF THE STORY: The Sunshine Company plane was rising above lightning and torrential rain on its way to Reno when its engines apparently failed.

7. LEAD: Several US industries are experiencing the effects of NAFTA.

   REST OF THE STORY: Asparagus growers are finding that more fresh asparagus is being imported from Mexico because of cheaper prices.

8. LEAD: Even the North is no escape from hot weather this week.

   REST OF THE STORY: According to the National Weather Service, temperatures in northern Arizona will remain in the scorching three digits.

9. LEAD: Three area people were killed in two separate highway accidents this Labor Day.

   REST OF THE STORY: A DeWitt construction worker was killed when a truck driver fell asleep and his semi slid into Jackson Perlini's [PER-leenee's] southbound lane on Highway 127 in Fullbright. The driver of the truck, Joey McCabe, was uninjured.

   Two Holt sisters were pronounced dead on arrival at Community Hospital after a drunk driver crossed the median on Interstate 69, just south of Eagle River. . . .

Name _____   Class _____   Date _____

10. LEAD: A police officer in New York has quit his job in deference to his principles.

   REST OF THE STORY: At a press conference in Manlius today, Jesse Morales called the judicial process a revolving door penal system.

EXERCISE 3: Writing Broadcast Stories

INSTRUCTIONS: Write broadcast stories about the following events. Write at least one soft news, one hard news and one throwaway lead. Check for wordiness. Your stories should not run more than 30 seconds. Correct any errors in style, spelling and grammar.

1. Previously, anyone who parked in a spot reserved for the handicapped in your city would be fined $20. However, your city council met last night and heard complaints that other motorists often use the spaces, making it harder for handicapped people to shop or eat out or go to movies. As a result, the council voted 5–2 to raise the fine to $250—the highest in the state—to discourage able-bodied drivers from using the parking spots reserved for the handicapped. Those spaces normally are close to store entrances. Two members of the Paralyzed Veterans Association were at the meeting to lobby for the stiffer fine, saying it might be the only way to stop offenders. The new law will go into effect in 30 days. State law allows half of the money collected through such fines to go toward enforcing and administering the parking regulations. The rest may be used to build wheelchair ramps and other improvements to enhance access to public buildings.

2. J. T. Pinero is a developer in your community. He is planning to build 350 houses in a 120-acre subdivision which he has named "Deer Run." This morning he was cited by the city. The city also stopped all work on the development. The land had been wooded, and Pinera was charged with clearing the first 30 acres without obtaining city permits. Mayor Serena Datolli said it was the most flagrant violation of the citys tree protection code since her election five years ago. Pinero was cited for cutting down more than 500 pines, oaks, maple, birch and other trees. Under city codes, unauthorized destruction of of each tree is punishable by a fine of up to $500. Datoli added that she and other city officials are negotiating with Pinero and his attorney for landscaping and replacement of all the trees. Pinero must also post a $100,000 bond or letter of credit to ensure restoration. If the work is done, Datoli said, Pinero might not be fined for this, his first offense. Pinaro said he did not know of the land-clearing and tree-removal permits required by the city.

3. Liz Holton operates a doughnut shop at 2240 Broadway Avenue. Today she was ordered to appear in court at 10 a.m. tomorrow morning. One of her employees is Mildred McCartey. Ms. McCartey was called for jury duty on Monday of last week and served the entire week. When she returned to work at 7 a.m. Monday of this week she found that she had been replaced, fired because of her absence last week. State law prohibits an employer from firing or threatening to fire an employee called for jury duty, and Judge George C. LeClair has ordered Liz to appear in his courtroom to determine whether she should be held in contempt of court. Interviewed today, Liz said she did not know of the

Name _____   Class _____   Date _____

law and never knew of it. She said she works 12 to 16 hours a day in the doughnut shop, which she owns. McCartney is her only full-time employee, and she said she cannot afford to have her away for several days at a time—she is unable to run the business by herself with only her part-time help. If held in contempt, she could be fined up to $10,000 and sentenced to six months in jail.

4. Wesley Barlow is an inmate in a Nebraska state prison. He has been charged with swindling dozens of widows out of thousands of dollars. Barlew, 32, is serving an 8-year sentence for burglary. Today he pleaded guilty to new charges against him and was sentenced to an additional 10 years on top of the old sentence. Barlow had mailed letters to men who recently died not long ago. The letters were then received by the mens widows. The letters sought payment—usually less than $100—"for maintenance and repairs." Some women paid because they assumed their dead husbands had some work done before their deaths, a detective thought. Barlow said he got their names from the obituaries in an Omaha newspaper. The scam was discovered when the mother of an Omaha detective received one of the letters.

5. Researchers at your college issued a report today. After three years of study, they confirmed the widely assumed link between drinking and birth defects. They warned that pregnant women who drink risk injury to their children. Because the scientists don't know how much alcohol may be safely consumed by pregnant women, they recommend absolute and total abstention from all alcoholic beverages during a womans 9-month term of pregnancy. What the doctors found during their three years of study is that children born to pregnant women who drink have higher rates of mental and physical abnormalities. The most common problems among such infants are mental retardation and delays in their physical development. Pregnant women who drink also experience more miscarriages and premature births. The reason for the problems is that alcohol from a mothers system passes directly into the bloodstream of her developing child, and that the alcohol remains in the fetal system longer because it is not metabolized and excreted as fast as it is by an adult. Scientists call the problem the fetal alcohol syndrome.

EXERCISE 4: Writing Shorter Broadcast Stories

INSTRUCTIONS: Write broadcast stories about the following events. Write at least one soft news, one hard news and one throwaway lead. Check for wordiness. Although you may find it difficult at first, limit your stories to 20 seconds or less. Correct any errors in style, spelling and grammar.

1. Although three straight national girls' marbles champions have come from your city, it gives them no place to play or practice. Their coach, whos Cheryl Nichols, is looking for donations to build marble shooting rings. "If we had rings, then we could recruit more kids and turn out more champions," said Cheryl. "And, it would be great for tourism." Cheryl is a an avid supporter of the sport. She won the 1980 national championship and has coached the last 7 out of 10 winners, including Tim Onn

and Wendy Jaco, of your city, who won this years championship. To practice, the kids must use portable rings or go to LaSage, which is forty minutes away. Some kids have parents who cannot travel the distance on a regular basis. Cheryl said that it takes several years and about 4,000 hours of practice to make a champion. Cheryl thinks it would cost about $700 to build a ring—a 14 × 14 foot smooth, concrete pad—and that at least 4 are necessary. Donated materials and labor would lower the cost.

2. The state has initiated a new drug program and is happy with the response. The new drug program is to help low-income Medicare folks buy prescription drugs at reduced prices. "We are happy with the early response," said Edwin diMarco, your states health secretary. The State Pharmacy Discount Program was approved by the state legislature about 3 years ago, and was finally inacted at the beginning of this month. People who can take advantage of the program are Medicare recipients with incomes up to 175% of the federal poverty level—$15,715 for an individual or $21,210 for a family of two. Members already get a 15% discounted price that the state negotiates with pharmaceutical manufacturers for the Medicaid program. The new program enables them to get a 35% discount off of that. Edwin says that this is a substantial savings. The problem, he says, is that a majority of people who are eligible havent enrolled yet. The challenge is to get the word out. About 4 thousand elderly citizens have enrolled, although the state estimates 50,000 citizens are eligible for the program. He is using Dr.'s offices and senior citizen centers to spread the word. Prescription drugs is a very high concern for seniors. To inquire about the program, request an application or just talk to someone about it, you can call toll free 1-800-444-2692.

3. From 11 at night to 4 in the morning, people more easily can pick up or drop off airline passengers at the airport. Community Capital Airport is now offering free parking for drivers and their passengers. "You must park in the hourly garage and only between those times," said Sherman Kirpatrick, the director of the airport. They will not be having police officers there to check your vehicle. If you mess up where you park, then you have to pay that area's full fees. If you park earlier or later than the designated times, then you must pay the full price of $8 an hour. The airport and the airlines are trying to encourage people to travel at all times of the day and night. And, they are trying to make it a nicer experience for night travelers and their drivers.

4. The police have not identified a suspect or motive, but the physician—Richardo Cessarini—who was shot Tuesday evening about 7 p.m. in his driveway—on Cypress Blvd.—has now died—at Community Hospital, where he has been in critical condition since the shooting. Before he died it was not a homicide case, but now authorities say it is. Cessarini was shot, in the head, as he got out of his 2002 Mercedes. His wallet and other items on him were not taken. The police have been questioning neighbors, looking for clues. They are following up on a tip that a light colored Navigator was seen leaving the scene. Cessarini was described by family and friends as a kind, loving father and a giving doctor who had time for everyone.

5. The city hopes to save about $3 million this year in its first stage of a new program that it hopes could eventually save 10 times that amount in the future. The mayor said she hopes to do this through bulk buying and consolidation of contracts. "We should manage our spending—buy in bulk—just like families do and operate our budget— including consolidating our contracts—just like a Fortune 500 company does." Mayor Datoli noted, for example, that the city had 30 different contracts for buying computers and software and 40 different contracts for janitorial supplies. "That's changed," she says. Also, with bulk buying, things cost less: a whole puncher used to cost $11.57, and now costs $5.03; a 100 watt light bulb that had cost $0.42 now costs $0.21. However, citizens should not expect to see this savings reflected in lower city taxes. "This savings will be applied to reducing the budget's deficit," said Tony Ferguson, the City Treasurer.

EXERCISE 5: Writing Broadcast Stories from More Facts

INSTRUCTIONS: Write broadcast stories about the following topics. Write at least one soft news, one hard news and one throwaway lead. Check for wordiness. Your stories should not run more than 30 seconds. Correct any errors in style, spelling and grammar.

1. The citys Board of Education met at 8 p.m. yesterday in the board headquarters. The board considered four proposals. First it awarded Certificates of Appreciation to 17 retiring teachers. Second it approved the appointment of Reba Caravel, now vice principal at Central High School, to principal of Martin Luther King Jr. High School. Third it approved a proposal to let individual high school PTAs decide whether or not to require school uniforms. And fourth it approved a 3.6% raise for all teachers and administrators. "We'll be trading designer jeans and stylish shirts and $200 sneakers for blue-and-white uniforms," said Priscilla Eisen, president of the Kennedy High School PTA. "Everyone favors this. Jumpers or skirts and blouses for girls and trousers, shirts and ties for every boy." Thus, the city will join a small but growing number of public schools nationwide hanging up fashion trends. Supt. Gerrie Hubbard said uniforms may not be suitable for every public school, but it will benefit students, since uniforms are an equalizer, a way to make poor kids indistinguishable from more affluent kids, and a way to end a clothes competition that seems to dominate some schools. "We're not interested in the best-dressed child here," said Hubard. "We're interested in emphasizing achievement and raising self-esteem. We want to stop concentration on clothes and start concentration on basic skills." School officials hope the idea may also be a unifier, creating more of a sense of togetherness and also instill a greater pride in school. "We decided we needed something to bring everyone together. It also imposes discipline and reduces thefts, especially of clothing. And it alleviates a lot of financial problems for parents. Kids can be cruel," Hubard said. "They'll make fun of someone who's wearing $9.99 Kmart specials instead of $95 Gloria Vanderbilts. Uniforms take a lot of pressure off the kids and parents." The uniforms will cost about $30 each, and provisions will be made for students who can't afford to buy three of them.

2. Its a tragedy being investigated in your city. Your city has many homes for the elderly, including Elder Haven at 1040 Broughton Drive. In the last 3 months alone 4

Name _____ **Class** _____ **Date** _____

residents of the home passed away. Today, the citys social service agencies announced they are launching an investigation into the deaths. A team of doctors and nurses will look into why 4 residents of the state-licensed manor died and whether the deaths could have been prevented. Two died while suffering from severe bed sores and urinary infections. A watchdog group, your states Department of Health and Rehabilitative Services, inspects nursing homes, normally once a year, and gave the home a rating last year of "marginally acceptable," citing numerous problems to clear up. People wonder whether social workers for the department could have prevented the deaths. Critics say the department failed to act in time. The first incident being investigated occurred 3 months ago when a 85 year old resident was admitted to a local hospital. He was dehydrated, his body temperature dangerously low, and his body covered by bruises and bed sores. He died a week later. Six weeks ago city inspectors found two other patents who needed "immediate medical attention." One was a 69-year-old woman, the other a 76-year-old man, and both eventually died. Yet another woman died just last week.

3. Sara Howard of 812 Bell Av. is a hero. She has the bad burns to prove it. "It wasn't that big a deal," she said to you. Police officer Howard, 28, was on routine patrol, starting her shift at 7 a.m. today. Her first call concerned a car-truck collision on Heritage Road. Gas was spewing from the cars punctured fuel tank, and Howard could see that three women were inside. "I just waited for an opening in the flames and then went for the door," Howard said. Three times the officer charged the car and three times was driven back by the raging, hot, fiery flames. Howard then proceeded to empty an extinguisher in her car on the flames and two of the women were able to get out largely under their own power but in the backseat was 78-year-old Suzanne Kopp. Howard, feeling the searing heat along her left side, finally succeeded in grabbing the woman and tugged her to safety. They looked back and "the whole car was just a total fireball," a witness at the scene said. Other witnesses at the scene were awestruck. "How many people would go into a car completely engulfed?" asked Charles Kalani, another witness. "Not very many, I think." None of the women in the car was badly hurt but Howard ended up in Regional Medical Center with serious 2nd and 3rd burns on her left side from her ankle to her arm and face. She remains hospitalized and will miss at least a week of work, maybe a month. "I just hope that somebody would do the same thing if it were my parents or grandmother in her car," Howard said. Her boss, Police Chief Bary Kopperud said the women in the burning car were lucky Howard drove by. "She's really brave," Kopperuud said. "It didn't surprise me a bit what she did, and I've recommended her for our Medal of Valor—its the highest award we give—for risking her life to save others."

4. In the past citys have offered cash for guns and the response has been good. Police in those cities have collected hundreds, sometimes thousands, of guns, mostly pistols which they want to get off the streets, but also rifles and shotguns. Now your city is planning a new program called "Toys for Guns." Anyone who turns in a gun will be given a gift certificate worth $100 at Toys R Us. Local businessmen are providing the

money. They hope people will give up their guns to get toys for their kids, especially at Christmas. So far the program has received a significant amount in donations and expects much, much more. "Its a simple solution to a serious problem" says local businessman Minny Cosby, who thought of the idea. "You have to put something in a persons hands once you take something out of their hands." There are an estimated 200 million firearms in the U.S. In other cities people have been given football tickets, a choice of sporting events, rock concerts or fancy restaurant meals. Critics say most guns collected are from law-abiding citizens, not criminals. "If you get even one gun off the street you may prevent a tragedy," Cosby responds however. "Besides, if honest people turn in their guns, they can't be stolen. That's where a lot of criminals get their guns." The police promise to ask no questions and to destroy the guns. Cosby proposed the idea at a recent regular monthly meeting of the citys Chamber of Commerce and other people in attendance at the meeting immediately pledged additional contributions which has thus far reached a grand total of $43,500 and is still growing.

5. Lynn Aneja is a 14-year-old teen-ager. She is the daughter of Mr. and Mrs. David Aneja, 489 Tulip. Her father is a deputy sheriff with the county sheriffs department. Her mother is a homemaker known for volunteering much of her time—20 or more hours a week—to help the homeless in your city by running a soup kitchen for the hungry and homeless at Calvary Assembly of God Church. Lynn, an only child, told police that her dad came to her bedroom last night where she was studying at about 10 p.m. and said goodnight and that he loved her very much and hugged her. Earlier, she said, she'd heard her parents arguing. Minutes after her dad left her room Lynn heard a series of shots, one after the other. She ran to her parents bedroom. Both were dead. She promptly dialed 911. Police responding to her call found two bloody dead bodies in the bedroom: her mothers and her fathers in separate pools of blood. Sheriff Gus DeCessari said in a press conference this morning: "Its hard, these tragedies, hard on everyone: the family, neighbors, co-workers, everyone. David was a 17-year veteran and was recently promoted from corporal to sergeant." A preliminary investigation suggests that David shot his wife three times, then turned the gun on himself, firing a single gunshot into his open mouth. Both were dead when police arrived on the scene. The investigation is continuing, and autopsies are scheduled for today. Mrs. Aneja was struck twice in the chest and once in the left arm. The daughter, Lynn, is staying with neighbors. Sheriff DeCessari said David had an exemplary record, and no one knows any reason for the murder/suicide apparently committed with Davids service revolver.

Name _____   Class _____   Date _____

EXERCISE TO ACCOMPANY CHAPTER 14

Visual Journalism

EXERCISE 1: Video Journalism Project

INSTRUCTIONS: Select a video embedded in a news story or one that stands alone. Choose something connected to a news event, a controversial issue or a feature story. Analyze the video by applying the following questions.

- What do you see?
- What story is the photographer trying to tell?
- What message is he or she sending? Is the photograph conveying it successfully? Why or why not?
- Does it dramatize, emphasize, or help summarize the story? Give details to explain your answer.
- Why do you think the photographer chose that particular scene to capture and explain the story? Why do you think the photo editor and editor selected the photo or photos for publication?

Name _____   Class _____   Date _____

EXERCISES TO ACCOMPANY CHAPTER 15

Speeches and Meetings

EXERCISE 1: Speeches

INSTRUCTIONS: Write separate advance and follow stories about each of the following speeches. Because the speeches are reprinted verbatim, you may quote them directly. Correct all errors.

1. FIREFIGHTER CONCERNS

Information for Advance Story

Tony Sullivan is scheduled to speak to the Downtown Rotary Club Monday of next week. The club meets every Monday noon at the Blackhawk Hotel. Lunch is served and costs $8.50 per person. The public is invited to the lunch, which begins promptly at noon, or the public may come for just the speech, which will begin promptly at 1 p.m. Tony Sullivan is your city's fire chief, and he will speak to the club members about the major concerns of today's firefighters.

Speech for Follow Story

Some of you don't know me. My name is Tony Sullivan. When I was 22 years old and had just been discharged from the Army, I didn't know what I wanted to do with the rest of my life. Two of my best friends wanted to join the Fire Department, and they talked me into taking all the physical and written tests along with them. I passed, but they didn't, and I've been associated with the Fire Department for the past 28 years. For the past 6 years, I've been chief.

The Fire Department is much different today than it was when I joined 28 years ago, and we've got much different problems today. I've been asked to talk to you about those problems. Our biggest problems, as you might expect, are low pay and long hours. But we're also concerned about the problems of arson and outdated gear. Now I'd like to talk to you about each of those problems, and in much more detail. As local business people, all of you are affected by the problems, and I hope that you'll be able to help us solve them.

First, the problem of arson. Its gotten completely out of hand. Property owners in this state alone lost at least $1 billion in damaged and destroyed property due to arson last year. We'd estimate, conservatively, that right here in this city 10 to 20 percent of our fires are arson. Its hard to control because the conviction rate for arson is low. And that's because fires oftentimes destroy the evidence. You, as business people, lose money because arson causes higher insurance premiums for everyone. It also causes lower profits, lost wages to workers, and lost tax revenue to the city.

Another big problem we face involves the gear we use in fighting fires. A good truck these days costs $300,000. If we want a good ladder truck, one that can reach some of the taller downtown buildings, it may cost twice that much. The city can't afford many, but if we don't have the trucks, then we can't rescue people trapped on the upper floors of those buildings.

Even the protective gear worn by our firefighters is getting terribly expensive. Until recently, all our protective clothing has been made of a highly flammable cotton coated with neoprene, usually black. Black is bad because it absorbs heat and because firefighters can't be seen if they fall and get into trouble inside a dark building or a building filled with smoke. Then take a look at our helmets; they're far from being the state of the art. They melt in temperatures above 700. In your average fire, the floor temperature is 200 and

Name _____ Class _____ Date _____

the ceiling is 1,800. The state-of-the-art helmets can resist heat up to 2,000 degrees, but they cost three times what we're paying now.

One reason why the injury and death rate among firefighters is so high—more firefighters die annually than police—is because our gear is so expensive, and cities won't buy it. They seem to think it's easier to replace firefighters than to outlay the money for better gear.

The heavy physical labor and working conditions also contribute to the high injury rate. When you send people into a fire, and you've got intense heat, broken glass, the danger of whole walls and floors collapsing, and the danger of explosions from unknown chemicals stored in these buildings, its almost inevitable that you're going to have some injuries and possibly even some deaths. With the proper equipment, we could reduce the number and severity of injuries, but there's no way to completely eliminate them. Danger's a part of our job. We accept that.

Despite the fact that we have a higher death rate than the police, firefighters start out earning $2,000 to $3,000 a year less than they do, and we object to that. Its not fair. When we ask the City Council why, they say because it's always been that way and it would cost too much to pay firefighters as much as the police. We don't think that's right, especially when you consider that the police work only 40 hours a week. Firefighters work 24-hour shifts and an average of 56 hours a week. So they work longer hours for less money.

The next time you hear anyone talking about these problems, and the next time you see us going to the City Council, requesting a larger budget, we'd appreciate your support. With your support, we'll be able to offer you, and everyone else in the city, better fire protection. It's already good, but with your help we can make it even better, and that benefits everyone.

2. ABORTION CRITIC

Information for Advance Story

John F. Palladino is an outspoken critic of abortion. He is scheduled to speak at a prayer breakfast next Sunday at the First Baptist Church, 412 North Eastland Ave., in your city. His topic will be, "Abortion: Our Greatest Sin." The public is invited free of charge for both the breakfast and speech. The prayer breakfast will be held in the church's social hall, starting at 7:30 a.m. Palladino is a Republican and unsuccessful candidate for governor in the last election in your state. He was defeated in the Republican primary. Previously, he served three terms in your State Senate. Currently, he lives in the state capital and operates his own real estate firm there. He is chairman of your states Right to Life Committee, which opposes abortion.

Speech for Follow Story

I appreciate your invitation to speak to you today. I also appreciate the help that many of you have given our Right to Life Committee. I recognize that some of you have given us very generous financial donations, and that others of you have helped man our telephone lines and distribute our literature.

I'd like to begin this morning by telling you something of my personal views. Personally, I cannot understand how a woman can achieve sexual liberation by taking the life of her unborn child. I believe that abortion basically is a very selfish, self-centered remedy to those that think the birth of a child is an inconvenience. I think it is an inconvenience for only nine months. After that, there are 3- or 4-year waits to adopt children. I know of many families who go down to El Salvador to adopt children. I have other friends who adopted little babies from Korea and from many other countries of the world. So no child is unwanted; there's a loving home in this country for every child.

Now some people ask, "What about cases where the mothers life is threatened, or where the mother is impregnated through rape or incest?" My main concern is with the 99 percent of the abortions that do not deal with that, but merely with inconvenience. When the mother's life is in question, and its a true case of the life of a mother vs. the life of an unborn child, certainly the life of the mother should take precedence—the reason being that there is a good possibility that the mother is already a mother of other children. To say that we're going to deprive these already-born children of their mother to protect the life of an unborn child is improper.

But I find it difficult from a personal standpoint to say that I would agree to abortion in the case of rape or incest because, again, it's an innocent child no matter whether its the product of a legitimate or illegitimate sexual union. So if I had the authority to stop all abortions, except those that involve the endangerment of the mother's life, then certainly I would agree to that.

Now, in talking about this issue, you have to remember one critical point. Life begins upon fertilization of the egg. If you don't agree with that, certainly at least you have the potential for life at that point, and therefore it should be as jealously guarded as life itself.

The federal and state laws that permit abortion are wrong, absolutely and totally wrong. Abortions are a crime and a sin. When governments adopt these laws, they're saying that life doesn't exist, or that some forms of life aren't as important as others and don't deserve the same protection as others. So even from a political view, abortion is wrong because it allows governments to judge the value of life—to say that there's a point or condition under which some lives can be ended. I think that's a very dangerous position for government to be in. And you have to ask where it'll stop. What other lives will governments decide we can end? Next it could be the sick, the elderly, the insane or the criminals from all our jails. That's not the kind of decision government should be making. All life is precious. All life should be protected by the government—and by us, as individuals.

Thank you.

EXERCISE 2: Surgeon General's Speech

INSTRUCTIONS: Write a news story that summarizes the following speech given by the surgeon general of the U.S. Public Health Service. Assume that the surgeon general spoke at a state PTA convention in your city at 8 p.m. yesterday. This is a verbatim copy of a speech actually given by the surgeon general and can be quoted directly. As you write the story, assume that it is just a few days before Halloween. You can find the identity of the current surgeon general and background about that person at *https://www.surgeongeneral .gov/*. Correct all errors.

SPEECH

I am pleased to be here today with representatives of several organizations who recognize that alcohol is the nations number one drug problem among youth and who share my concern that the alcohol industry has targeted Halloween, a traditional holiday for children, as their latest marketing opportunity.

Just as Saman, the ancient Keltic Lord of the Dead, summoned the evil spirits to walk the earth on October 31, Americas modern day distilleries, breweries and vineyards are working their own brand of sorcery on us this year. On radio and television and even at supermarket check-out counters we are being bombarded with exhortations to purchase orange and black 12-packs and even "cocktails from the Crypt."

Well, as your surgeon general I'm here today with my own exhortation: Halloween and hops do not mix.

Name _____   Class _____   Date _____

Alcohol is the number one substance abuse problem among Americas youth. In fact, it is the only drug whose use has not been declining, according to our most recent National High School Senior Survey. The National Institute on Alcohol Abuse and Alcoholism reports that, currently, 4.6 million teen-agers have a drinking problem.

Why do so many of our young people drink? There are no easy answers to this question, but clearly the availability of alcohol and its acceptance, even glamorization, in our society are factors. The National Coalition on Television Violence reports that before turning 18, the average American child will see 75,000 drinking scenes on television programs alone.

In just two days many of our young people will be celebrating Halloween. Many children look forward to this day as much as they do Christmas and Hanukkah. Who among us can forget the excitement of dressing up as ghosts and goblins and going from door to door shouting "trick or treat," and coming away with a fistful of candy?

Trick or treat.

This year the alcohol industry has given new meaning to those innocent words of childhood. They are serving up new treats—and new tricks.

They are saying: "It's Halloween, it's time to celebrate, it's time for a drink!" Beer companies offer free Halloween T-shirts, bat sunglasses, and glowing cups. Halloween parties sponsored by a major brewer are being held in nearly 40 cities.

What I say is scary is the possibility of increased carnage on our highways, the real specter of more binge drinking by our young people, and the absolute reality of those smaller, less dramatic cases of health and emotional problems caused by alcohol consumption.

Last year alone, we lost 3,158 young people in alcohol-related crashes, over 60 in every state in the union. Fully 40 percent of all deaths in young people are due to crashes—6,649 last year, and, as you can see, about half are related to alcohol.

What is also scary to me is the encouragement of "binge drinking" by our young people. Some of these Halloween ads encourage the purchase of 12 or 24 packs of beer, and who will drink all that beer? 43 percent of college students, 35 percent of our high school seniors and 26 percent of 8th grade students have had five or more drinks in a row during the past two weeks. And beer and wine coolers are their favorite alcoholic beverages.

I also find it scary that we continue to think of beer and wine as "soft liquor." There's nothing "soft" about ethyl alcohol. And there's just as much ethyl alcohol in one can of beer or one glass of wine as there is in a mixed drink. That is the hard fact.

Finally, as the nations doctor and as a pediatrician, what I find scariest of all is that alcohol affects virtually every organ in the body. Alcohol consumption is associated with medical consequences ranging from slight functional impairment to life-threatening disease states—among them, liver disease, cancer of the esophagus, and hypertension. Where the organs of the body are concerned, alcohol is an equal opportunity destroyer.

The alcohol industry and its hired guns, the advertising agencies, know these facts. I hope that parents and other concerned adults do, too. For if the alcohol industry has chosen to be part of the problem, it is up to you to be part of the solution.

In closing I would like to speak on behalf of those who have no voice in this debate—Americas children and adolescents. Let us not make this year, the year they robbed the kids of Halloween. For their sake and our own, let us keep Halloween sane, safe—and sober.

Name _____   Class _____   Date _____

EXERCISE 3: President Bill Clinton's Memorial Address for Oklahoma City Bombing Victims

INSTRUCTIONS: This is a transcript of President Bill Clinton's address at the memorial service held on April 23, 1995, for the people who died in the explosion that destroyed the Alfred P. Murrah Federal Building in Oklahoma City. The service was held at the State Fairgrounds Arena in Oklahoma City and was attended by more than 10,000 people. Oklahoma Gov. Frank Keating and the Rev. Billy Graham also spoke at the service. Because the speech is reprinted verbatim, you may quote it directly.

BACKGROUND: This information is what was known to the public on the day President Clinton gave this speech.

The Oklahoma City federal building had been destroyed by a bomb, made from fertilizer and fuel oil, that exploded the morning of April 19. The number of people known at this time to have died in the blast is 78. In addition, 432 people have been injured, and 150 are still missing. Soon after the explosion, FBI agents announced they were seeking two white men whom they were calling John Doe No. 1 and John Doe No. 2. The agents now suspect Timothy James McVeigh of Kingman, Ariz., is John Doe No. 1 and have charged him with destruction of federal property. Just hours after the bombing, McVeigh was arrested by an Oklahoma trooper for driving without a license plate and carrying a concealed knife. The search for John Doe No. 2 is continuing. FBI agents have been questioning Terry Nichols of Herington, Kan., and his brother James of Decker, Mich. Neither Terry nor James Nichols is suspected of being John Doe No. 2. But federal agents say in affidavits filed in court that the Nichols brothers and McVeigh are involved in right-wing militia organizations and know one another. Other court papers described McVeigh as angry with the federal government because of the assault by federal agents on the Branch Davidian complex in Waco, Texas, on April 19, 1993.

THE PRESIDENT'S SPEECH

Today our nation joins with you in grief. We mourn with you. We share your hope against hope that some may still survive. We thank all those who have worked so heroically to save lives and to solve this crime, those here in Oklahoma and those who are across this great land, and many who left their own lives to come here to work, hand-in-hand, with you.

We pledge to do all we can to help you heal the injured, to rebuild this city and to bring to justice those who did this evil.

This terrible sin took the lives of our American family, innocent children in that building only because their parents were trying to be good parents as well as good workers; citizens in the building going about their daily business; and many there who served the rest of us, who worked to help the elderly and the disabled, who worked to support our farmers and our veterans, who worked to enforce our laws and to protect us.

Let us say clearly they served us well and we are grateful.

But for so many of you, they were also neighbors and friends. You saw them at church, or the P.T.A. meetings, at the civic clubs or the ball park. You know them in ways that all the rest of America could not. And to all the members of the families here present who have suffered loss, though we share your grief, your pain is unimaginable and we know that. We cannot undo it. That is God's work.

Our words seem small beside the loss you have endured, but I found a few I wanted to share today. I have received a lot of letters in these last terrible days. One stood out because it came from a young widow and a mother of three whose own husband was murdered with over 200 other Americans when Pan Am 103 was shot down. Here is what that woman said I should say to you today.

"The anger you feel is valid but you must not allow yourselves to be consumed by it. The hurt you feel must not be allowed to turn into hate, but instead into the search for justice. The loss you feel must not paralyze your own lives. Instead, you must try to pay tribute to your loved ones by continuing to do all the things they left undone, thus ensuring they did not die in vain."

Wise words from one who also knows.

You have lost too much but you have not lost everything, and you have certainly not lost America, for we will stand with you for as many tomorrows as it takes.

If ever we needed evidence of that, I could only recall the words of Governor and Mrs. (Cathy) Keating, "If anybody thinks that Americans are mostly mean and selfish, they ought to come to Oklahoma."

If anybody thinks Americans have lost the capacity for love, and caring, and courage, they ought to come to Oklahoma.

To all my fellow Americans beyond this hall I say, one thing we owe those who have sacrificed is the duty to purge ourselves of the dark forces which gave rise to this evil.

There are forces that threaten our common peace, our freedom, our way of life. Let us teach our children that the God of comfort is also the God of righteousness. Those who trouble their own house will inherit the wind. Justice will prevail.

Let us let our own children know that we will stand against the forces of fear. When there is talk of hatred, let us stand up and talk against it. When there is talk of violence, let us stand up and talk against it. In the face of death let us honor life.

As St. Paul admonished us, "Let us not be overcome by evil, but overcome evil with good."

Yesterday Hillary and I had the privilege of speaking with some children of other federal employees, children like those who were lost here. And one little girl said something we will never forget. She said, "We should all plant a tree in memory of the children." So this morning before we got on the plane to come here, at the White House, we planted that tree in honor of the children of Oklahoma.

It was a dogwood with its wonderful spring flower and its deep enduring roots. It embodies the lesson of the Psalms that the life of a good person is like a tree whose leaf does not wither.

My fellow Americans, a tree takes a long time to grow, and wounds take a long time to heal, but we must begin. Those who are lost now belong to God. Some say we will be with them, but until that happens, their legacy must be our lives.

Thank you all and God bless you.

EXERCISE 4: Remarks by President Barack Obama at the 2016 Toner Prize Ceremony

INSTRUCTIONS: Write a news story summarizing this speech, which President Obama delivered at the awarding of the 2016 Toner Prize for political reporting. The text is verbatim and may be quoted directly. You should use the Internet to find background information about Robin Toner and the Toner Prize.

Andrew W. Mellon Auditorium
Washington, D.C.
7:49 P.M. EST

THE PRESIDENT:

It is a great honor to be here to celebrate the 2015 Toner Prize for Excellence in Political Reporting. In this political season, it is worth reflecting on the kind of journalism Robin practiced—and the kind of journalism this prize rewards.

A reporter's reporter—that was Robin. From her first job at the Charleston Daily Mail to her tenure as the New York Times' national political correspondent—the first woman to hold that position—she always saw herself as being a servant for the American public. She had a sense of mission and purpose in her work. For Robin, politics was not a horserace, or a circus, or a tally of who scored more political points than whom, but rather was fundamentally about issues and how they affected the lives of real people.

She treated the public with respect—didn't just skim the surface. Few reporters understood the intricacies of health care policy better. Few could cut to the heart of a tax reform plan more deeply—and analyze how it would affect everybody, from a struggling worker to a hedge fund manager. Few could explain complicated, esoteric political issues in a way that Americans could digest and use to make informed choices at the ballot box.

Robin's work was meticulous. No detail was too small to confirm, and no task too minor to complete. And that, too, she saw as her responsibility—the responsibility of journalism. She famously developed her own fact-checking system, cleaning up every name and date and figure in her piece—something most reporters relied on others to do. And it's no wonder then that of her almost 2,000 articles, only six required published corrections. And knowing Robin, that was probably six too many for her taste.

And this speaks to more than just her thoroughness or some obsessive compulsiveness when it came to typos. It was about Robin's commitment to seeking out and telling the truth. She would not stand for any stray mark that might mar an otherwise flawless piece—because she knew the public relied on her to give them the truth as best as she could find it.

Of course, these were qualities were harder to appreciate when her lens was focused on you. She held politicians' feet to the fire, including occasionally my own. And in her quiet, dogged way, she demanded that we be accountable to the public for the things that we said and for the promises that we made. We should be held accountable.

That's the kind of journalism that Robin practiced. That's the kind of journalism this prize honors. It's the kind of journalism that's never been more important. It's the kind of journalism that recognizes its fundamental role in promoting citizenship, and hence undergirds our democracy.

As I've said in recent weeks, I know I'm not the only one who may be more than a little dismayed about what's happening on the campaign trail right now. The divisive and often vulgar rhetoric that's aimed at everybody, but often is focused on the vulnerable or women or minorities. The sometimes well-intentioned but I think misguided attempts to shut down that speech. The violent reaction that we see, as well as the deafening silence from too many of our leaders in the coarsening of the debate. The sense that facts don't matter, that they're not relevant. That what matters is how much attention you can generate. A sense that this is a game as opposed to the most precious gift our Founders gave us—this collective enterprise of self-government.

And so it's worth asking ourselves what each of us—as politicians or journalists, but most of all, as citizens—may have done to contribute to this atmosphere in our politics. I was going to call is "carnival atmosphere," but that implies fun. And I think it's the kind of question Robin would have asked all of us. As I said a few weeks ago, some may be more to blame than others for the current climate, but all of us are responsible for reversing it.

I say this not because of some vague notion of "political correctness," which seems to be increasingly an excuse to just say offensive things or lie out loud. I say this not out of nostalgia, because politics in America has always been tough. Anybody who doubts that should take a look at what Adams and Jefferson and some of our other Founders said about each other. I say this because what we're seeing right now does corrode our democracy and our society. And I'm not one who's faint of heart. I come from Chicago. Harold Washington once explained that "politics ain't beanbag." It's always been rough and tumble.

Name _____   Class _____   Date _____

But when our elected officials and our political campaign become entirely untethered to reason and facts and analysis, when it doesn't matter what's true and what's not, that makes it all but impossible for us to make good decisions on behalf of future generations. It threatens the values of respect and tolerance that we teach our children and that are the source of America's strength. It frays the habits of the heart that underpin any civilized society—because how we operate is not just based on laws, it's based on habits and customs and restraint and respect. It creates this vacuum where baseless assertions go unchallenged, and evidence is optional. And as we're seeing, it allows hostility in one corner of our politics to infect our broader society. And that, in turn, tarnishes the American brand.

The number one question I am getting as I travel around the world or talk to world leaders right now is, what is happening in America—about our politics. And it's not because around the world people have not seen crazy politics; it is that they understand America is the place where you can't afford completely crazy politics. For some countries where this kind of rhetoric may not have the same ramifications, people expect, they understand, they care about America, the most powerful nation on Earth, functioning effectively, and its government being able to make sound decisions.

So we are all invested in making this system work. We are all responsible for its success. And it's not just for the United States that this matters. It matters for the planet.

Whether it was exposing the horrors of lynching, to busting the oil trusts, to uncovering Watergate, your work has always been essential to that endeavor, and that work has never been easy. And let's face it, in today's unprecedented change in your industry, the job has gotten tougher. Even as the appetite for information and data flowing through the Internet is voracious, we've seen newsrooms closed. The bottom line has shrunk. The news cycle has, as well. And too often, there is enormous pressure on journalists to fill the void and feed the beast with instant commentary and Twitter rumors, and celebrity gossip, and softer stories. And then we fail to understand our world or understand one another as well as we should. That has consequences for our lives and for the life of our country.

Part of the independence of the Fourth Estate is that it is not government-controlled, and media companies thereby have an obligation to pursue profits on behalf of their shareholders, their owners, and also has an obligation to invest a good chunk of that profit back into news and back into public affairs, and to maintain certain standards and to not dumb down the news, and to have higher aspirations for what effective news can do. Because a well-informed electorate depends on you. And our democracy depends on a well-informed electorate.

So the choice between what cuts into your bottom lines and what harms us as a society is an important one. We have to choose which price is higher to pay; which cost is harder to bear.

Good reporters like the ones in this room all too frequently find yourselves caught between competing forces, I'm aware of that. You believe in the importance of a well-informed electorate. You've staked your careers on it. Our democracy needs you more than ever. You're under significant financial pressures, as well.

So I believe the electorate would be better served if your networks and your producers would give you the room, the capacity to follow your best instincts and dig deeper into the things that might not always be flashy, but need attention.

And Robin proves that just because something is substantive doesn't mean it's not interesting. I think the electorate would be better served if we spent less time focused on the he said/she said back-and-forth of our politics. Because while fairness is the hallmark of good journalism, false equivalency all too often these days can be a fatal flaw. If I say that the world is round and someone else says it's flat, that's worth reporting, but you might also want to report on a bunch of scientific evidence that seems to support the notion that the world is round. And that shouldn't be buried in paragraph five or six of the article. (Applause.)

Name _____   Class _____   Date _____

A job well done is about more than just handing someone a microphone. It is to probe and to question, and to dig deeper, and to demand more. The electorate would be better served if that happened. It would be better served if billions of dollars in free media came with serious accountability, especially when politicians issue unworkable plans or make promises they can't keep. (Applause.) And there are reporters here who know they can't keep them. I know that's a shocking concept that politicians would do that. But without a press that asks tough questions, voters take them at their word. When people put their faith in someone who can't possibly deliver on his or her promises, that only breeds more cynicism.

It's interesting—this is a little going off script. But we still have our house in Chicago, and because Michelle, me and the kids had to leave so quickly, it's a little bit like a time capsule, especially my desk—which wasn't always very neat. So I've got old phone bills that I think I paid—(laughter)—but they're still sitting there. And for a long time, I had my old laptop with the AOL connection. But there's also these big stacks of newspapers from right before the election. And every time I go back, I have occasion to look back and read what I said at the time. And Lord knows I've made mistakes in this job, and there are areas where I've fallen short, but something I'm really proud of is the fact that, if you go back and see what I said in 2007 and you see what I did, they match up. (Applause.)

Now, part of the reason they match up is because in 2008, during the campaign, people asked me really tough questions about whether they'd match up. And we had to spend a lot of time worrying about whether what I said I could deliver on, and whether we believed it was true. And there was a price if you said one thing and then did something completely different. And the question is, in the current media environment, is that still true? Does that still hold?

I think Robin understood this because she asked those questions. She asked me some of those questions.

One of the reasons I ran for this office was to try and change the tone of our politics in Washington. And I remember back in early 2008—eight years ago this month—Robin wrote a story wondering whether I could; whether it was even possible. At the time, I probably thought the piece was fairly cynical. And while I still believe Americans are hungry for a better politics, as I've said several times now, one of my great regrets is that the tone of our politics has gotten worse. And I won't take all the responsibility for it, but I'll take some. We all own some of it. I'll take my share. But Robin asked that question. She cast a critical eye from the very beginning. And that was useful. Still is.

As I believe that that for all the sideshows of the political season, Americans are still hungry for truth, it's just hard to find. It's hard to wade through. The curating function has diminished in this smartphone age. But people still want to know what's true.

Think about it. Hollywood released films about getting stuck on Mars, and demolition derbies in a post-apocalyptic wasteland, and you even had Leo DiCaprio battling a grizzly bear. And yet it was a movie about journalists spending months meticulously calling sources from landlines, and poring over documents with highlighters and microfiche, chasing the truth even when it was hard, even when it was dangerous. And that was the movie that captured the Oscar for Best Picture.

I'm not suggesting all of you are going to win Oscars. But I am saying it's worth striving to win a Toner. (Applause.)

So, look, ultimately I recognize that the news industry is an industry—it's a business. There's no escaping the pressures of the industry and all its attendant constraints. But I also know that journalism at its best is indispensable—not in some abstract sense of nobility, but in the very concrete sense that real people depend on you to uncover the truth. Real people depend on getting information they can trust because they are giving over decision-making that has a profound effect on their lives to a bunch of people who are pretty remote and very rarely will they ever have the chance to ask that person a direct question,

Name _____ Class _____ Date _____

or be able to sort through the intricacies of the policies that will determine their wages or their ability to retire, or their ability to send their kid to college, or the possibility that their child will be sent to war.

These are folks who trust you when you tell them that there's a problem in their schools, or that their water has been poisoned, or that their political candidates are promoting plans that don't add up.

That's why the deep reporting, the informed questioning, the in-depth stories—the kind of journalism that we honor today—matters more than ever and, by the way, lasts longer than some slapdash Tweet that slips off our screens in the blink of an eye, that may get more hits todays, but won't stand up to the test of time. (Applause.) That's the only way that our democracy can work.

And as I go into my last year, I spend a lot of time reflecting on how this system, how this crazy notion of self-government works; how can we make it work. And this is as important to making it work as anything—people getting information that they can trust, and that has substance and evidence and facts and truth behind it. In an era in which attention spans are short, it is going to be hard because you're going to have to figure out ways to make it more entertaining, and you're going to have to be more creative, not less. Because if you just do great reporting and nobody reads it, that doesn't do anybody any good, either.

But 10, 20, 50 years from now, no one seeking to understand our age is going to be searching the Tweets that got the most retweets, or the post that got the most likes. They'll look for the kind of reporting, the smartest investigative journalism that told our story and lifted up the contradictions in our societies, and asked the hard questions and forced people to see the truth even when it was uncomfortable.

Many of you are already doing that, doing incredible work. And in some ways, the new technologies are helping you do that work. Journalists are using new data techniques to analyze economics and the environment, and to analyze candidates' proposals. Anchors are asking candidates exactly how they're going to accomplish their promises, pressing them so they don't evade the question. Some reporters recently watched almost five hours of a certain candidate's remarks to count the number of times he said something that wasn't true. It turned out to be quite a large number. So talk about taking one for the team. That was a significant sacrifice they made.

This is journalism worth honoring and worth emulating. And to the young aspiring journalist that I had a chance to meet before I came on stage, those are the models you want to follow.

As all of you know, I just came back from Cuba, where I held a press conference with President Castro that was broadcast all over the country. So in a country without a free press, this was big news. And it was a remarkable thing that the Cuban people were able to watch two leaders—their own, and the leader of a country that they'd grown up understanding as their archenemy—answer tough questions and be held accountable. And I don't know exactly what it will mean for Cuba's future. I think it made a big difference to the Cuban people. And I can't think of a better example of why a free press is so vital to freedom. (Applause.)

In any country, including our own, there will be an inherent tension between the President and the press. It's supposed to be that way. I may not always agree with everything you report or write. In fact, it's fair to say I do not. (Laughter.) But if I did, that would be an indication that you weren't doing your job.

I'll tell you—I probably maybe shouldn't do this, but what the heck, I'm in my last year. (Laughter.) I had an in-depth conversation with President Putin a while back about Syria and Ukraine. And he had read an article in The Atlantic that Jeff Goldberg had done about my foreign policy doctrine. And he said, well, I disagree with some of the things that you said in there. And Jeff is a remarkable journalist who I admire greatly, and all the quotes that were directly attributed to me in there I completely agreed with. I said, well, but some of the things that were shaped may not fully reflect all the nuance of my thoughts on the particular topic that President Putin was mentioning. But I pointed out to him, of course, that unlike you, Vladimir, I don't get to edit the piece before it's published. (Laughter and applause.)

So you are supposed to push those in power for more evidence and more access. You're supposed to challenge our assumptions. Sometimes I will find this frustrating. Sometimes I may not be able to share with you all of the context of decisions that I make. But I never doubt how much—how critical it is to our democracy for you to do that; how much I value great journalism. And you should not underestimate the number of times that I have read something that you did, and I have called somebody up and said, what's going on here? Because as Bob Gates told me when I first came in—I think it was my first or second week—I said, well, what advice do you have, Bob? You've been around seven presidents. You've served in Washington, in the administration. He said, Mr. President, the only thing I can tell you for sure is that you've got about two million employees, and at any given moment in any given day, somebody, somewhere, is screwing up. (Laughter.)

So you help me do my job better, and I'm grateful for that. Because the point of politics, as Robin understood it—certainly as I've tried to understand it throughout my tenure in this job—the point of politics is not simply the amassing of power. It's about what you do with that power that has been lent to you through a compact, with a citizenry, who give you their proxy and say "I'm counting on you" to not just make my life better, but more importantly, to make my kids' lives better, and my grandkids' lives better. Who will we help? How will we help them? What kind of country do we leave to the next generation?

My hope is, is that you continue to ask us questions that keep us honest and elevate our democracy. I ask that you continue to understand your role as a partner in this process. I say this often when I speak to Democratic partisan crowds: I never said, "Yes, I can." I said, "Yes, we can." And that means all of us. (Applause.) If we can keep supporting the kind of work that Robin championed, if we cultivate the next generation of smart, tough, fair-minded journalists, if we can all, every single one of us, carry on her legacy of public service and her faith in citizenry—because you have to have a certain faith to be a really good journalist; you have to believe that me getting it right matters, that it's not just sending something into the void, but that there's somebody on the other end who's receiving it, and that matters—if you continue to believe that, if you have faith, I have no doubt that America's best days are ahead.

So thank you to Robin's family. Congratulations to this year's winner. And thank all of you. God bless you, and God bless the United States of America. (Applause.) Thank you.

END
8:22 P.M. EST

EXERCISE 5: County Commission Meeting

INSTRUCTIONS: Assume that your county commission held a meeting at 2 p.m. yesterday. Write a news story that summarizes the comments and decisions made at this meeting. Correct all errors.

The members of your county commission began their meeting by listening to plans for a luxury condominium development on Elkhart Lake. The new development will be called "SunCrest." The property is owned by the Roswell Development Corporation, headquartered in Pittsburgh. Carlos Rey, a spokesman for the company, said: "We are planning a series of 10-story buildings overlooking the lake. None will exceed 100 feet in height. They will contain a total of 715 units. Estimated selling price of a unit will be $250,000 and upwards, perhaps to a top of $750,000 for the larger penthouse units. The development is about 5 miles from the nearest town, and we intend to promote it as a vacation and recreation center. We'll have our own well and our own sewer system, with an extensive recreation system centered around the lake. We know

Name _____ Class _____ Date _____

that fire protection is a concern. The township fire department serving the area doesn't have a ladder truck capable of reaching the top of a 10-story building. We'll donate $600,000 for the purchase of one." The commission voted 5–2 to approve the plans and to rezone the land from agricultural to PUD: Planned Unit Development.

Next, at 3 p.m., the commission honored and presented plaques to two 15-year-old girls. The girls, Doreen Nicholls and Pamela DeZinno, were walking along a river in a county park last week and saw a young child fall from a boat. Both girls dove into the river and pulled her out. While Doreen then proceeded to administer CPR, Pamela called for help, thus saving a life.

Appearing next before the commission, Sheriff Gus DiCesare asked it to require a three-day wait before a pistol could be bought from any gun dealer in the county. "I do not think that 72 hours is too long for someone to wait to buy a handgun," Sheriff DiCesare said. "There are a lot of cases where people went out and bought a gun with criminal intent and used it right away to shoot or rob someone. We want a cooling off period." Under the proposed ordinance, a customer would have to provide the dealer with his name, address, date of birth and other information, then wait 72 hours before picking up the pistol. The dealer would mail the information to the sheriff's department, where it would be kept on a computerized file. Sheriff DiCesare said it would speed the identification of the owner of a pistol found at a crime scene. A majority of the commissioners said they favor such a proposal but want to get more information and possibly hold a public hearing to give every citizen an opportunity to speak his mind. They promised to seriously consider it at their next meeting.

The commissioners then decided not to give themselves a raise, rejecting a proposed pay raise on a 4–3 vote. It has been five years since the last pay raise for them. Then their salary went from $47,500 to $51,000 a year. Yesterday, the majority, led by Commissioners Roland Graumann and Anita Shenuski, argued that a raise was "inappropriate." Faith Ellis argued a proposed increase to $56,500 was not out of line because commissioners in other counties earn more. "This is not asking too much," she said. "The county is getting a good deal for the time we put in." Anne Chen responded, "Our work should be done for community service, not just for how much we make."

EXERCISE 6: City Council Hearing on Proposed Ordinance

INSTRUCTIONS: Your city council is considering a proposed ordinance that would restrict picketing in the vicinity of churches or other religious institutions before or after worship services. The ordinance is motivated by concerns expressed by congregants of a church that has been the target of antiabortion picketing. The council is holding a hearing on the proposed ordinance preparatory to voting on whether to adopt it. Using the background information and the statements of the people who testified for and against the proposed ordinance, write a news story summarizing the meeting. Material in quotation marks is verbatim and may be quoted directly. Correct all errors.

BACKGROUND

For 17 months, Regional Rescue, a group of antiabortion protesters, has been picketing Redeemer Lutheran Church, 822 Bell Avenue. The protesters have targeted this church because Dr. Priscilla Eisen, the only physician in your town who performs abortions, is a member of the church and a member of its council. The protesters always carry large signs with full-color photographs of aborted and dismembered fetuses. Some members of the church, especially those with young children, say they have been harassed by the protesters. Some members have left the church to avoid having to face the protesters every Sunday. Church leaders have worked with a local attorney, Enrique Diaz, to draft a proposed ordinance that would force the picketers with the large signs to stay across the street from the church.

The proposed ordinance says:

"A. For the purpose of this ordinance, 'focused picketing' means the act of one or more persons stationing herself, himself or themselves outside religious premises on the exterior grounds, or on the sidewalks, streets or other part of the right of way in the immediate vicinity of religious premises, or moving in a repeated manner past or around religious premises, while displaying a banner, placard, sign or other demonstrative material as part of their expressive conduct.

"B. It shall be deemed an unlawful disturbance of the peace for any person intentionally or knowingly to engage in focused picketing of a scheduled religious activity at any time within the period from one-half hour before to one-half hour after the scheduled activity, at any place (1) on the religious organization's exterior premises, including its parking lots; or (2) on the portion of the right of way including any sidewalk on the same side of the street and adjoining the boundary of the religious premises, including its parking lots; or (3) on the portion of the right of way adjoining the boundary of the religious premises which is a street or roadway including any median within such street or roadway; or (4) on any public property within 50 feet of a property boundary line of the religious premises, if an entrance to the religious organization's building or an entrance to its parking lot is located on the side of the property bounded by that property line. Notwithstanding the foregoing description of areas where focused picketing is restricted, it is hereby provided that no restriction in this ordinance shall be deemed to apply to focused picketing on the right of way beyond the curb line completely across the street from any such religious premises."

FIRST SPEAKER

Enrique Diaz, attorney representing Redeemer Lutheran Church and its members, speaks in favor of the ordinance

He uses two charts in his presentation. One is a diagram of what speech is protected by the First Amendment to the U.S. Constitution. The other chart lists and describes the criteria for constitutionally permissible restrictions on speech in public forums, such as public streets, sidewalks and parks.

"We know that there are two principle issues at stake here tonight. The first is whether the members of the Redeemer Lutheran Church have exaggerated the harm the picketers have caused. We've brought some families here tonight to describe what they've suffered so that you can hear for yourselves the seriousness of the harm. The second is whether an ordinance such as we propose is constitutional or whether requiring the picketers to go across the street violates their rights.

"Freedom of speech has never been deemed absolute by a majority of the U.S. Supreme Court. The exceptions to that freedom have been written around the edges. [Diaz points to the first of his charts.]

"This chart shows the field labeled American Freedoms of Speech and Press. Around the outside are the exceptions to those freedoms: obscenity, libel, invasion of privacy, copyright violations, fighting words, incitement to criminal riots, national security and time, place and manner regulations of public forums. It's the last of those exceptions, the regulation of public forums, that is at issue here.

"The Supreme Court has said that speech in a public forum may be restricted if the restrictions are content neutral, narrowly tailored, serve a significant governmental interest and leave open ample alternative channels of communication." [Diaz points to these criteria listed on his second chart.]

"The proposed ordinance is content neutral; it applies to all picketers regardless of what message they want to convey. And narrow tailoring is what this ordinance is about. Only picketing with placards, banners and signs and only at certain times and places would be restricted. The ordinance also leaves open alternative channels of expression. Protesters can show their banners, placards and signs from across the street, or they can protest on the sidewalks around the church if they don't use placards, banners and signs.

"The only question left is whether there is a significant government interest. The families you will hear testify will establish that. What's been going on around Redeemer Lutheran Church is a mechanism that restricts the right to worship. By targeting families with small children, the picketers with their graphic signs have been putting pressure on those children to persuade their parents to worship elsewhere. I say to Regional Rescue, 'You're hurting people and it's not fair. Picket on people your own size.'"

SECOND SPEAKER

Brenda DiVitini, 313 Coble Drive, assistant minister of Redeemer Lutheran Church

"The small children who come to our church are not just unfortunate victims. They are intentionally targeted by the antiabortion picketers. Photographs showing decapitated fetuses are held up to their car windows as their parents enter and leave the church parking lot.

"Children have been spiritually and emotionally harmed. Families have been forced to choose between attending the church of their choice and protecting their children. And there is no end to this in sight.

"The church is being held hostage by terrorists whose demands it cannot meet. The protesters have said they won't stop even if Dr. Eisen resigns as a council member and leaves the church. Only two things can cause Regional Rescue to quit picketing the church: Dr. Eisen stops performing abortions, or Redeemer Lutheran Church must publicly shun and condemn Dr. Eisen. Neither condition can be met by Redeemer Lutheran Church. We cannot control Priscilla Eisen's vocation, and our denomination does not allow shunning members."

THIRD SPEAKER

Diana Gant, 801 Village Lane, a member of the council of Redeemer Lutheran Church and a professor of psychology at the university

"This focused picketing at Redeemer Lutheran Church harms young children. They are vulnerable to the gruesome signs and adult conflict, especially when it involves them and those who care for them.

"A child's capacity for coping is limited. They can't regulate their emotions. They are more likely to be overcome. The picketers are exploiting the children's vulnerability.

"The antiabortion picketing is undermining families and the church as a safe haven. The children can't go to church without confronting the picketers from whom parents cannot protect them. This causes the children to experience profound anxiety. Any of you who an remember feeling defenseless in front of a threatening adult knows this. Studies support this personal experience.

"Government has a special responsibility to protect children, and the proposed ordinance allows the city to protect children and the constitutional rights of worshipers."

FOURTH SPEAKER

Carolyn Slater, 8443 Turkey Hollow, a former member of the Redeemer Lutheran Church

"My husband and I have two children, 7 and 10 years old. We left Redeemer Lutheran Church two months ago. Over the last year and a half we tried to minimize the impact of the harmful pictures these protesters carry. Our children felt fear and confusion when we took them to church. They felt threatened. When we went to church, we had our children ride on the floor of the van so they would not have to see the pictures. Every week, the children worried that they would have to see those pictures again.

"The police and city attorney say the picketers are peaceful and orderly. They are when they are being observed, but their behavior changes when they are not.

"And the picketers are only there when children are likely to be attending. They're there for Christmas services and craft shows and other events that attract children, but they're never there for adults-only events, like board meetings.

"We both love the church and its members, so we did not take leaving lightly. But continuing at Redeemer Lutheran Church would have be subjecting our children to child abuse. If the city fails to pass this ordinance, it will be a victory for the picketers. For the city, it will be a tragedy."

FIFTH SPEAKER

Floyd & Rose Leidih, 1812 Dickins Av., members of Redeemer Lutheran Church.(Only Rose talked while her husband remained at her side, comforting her during the most emotional parts of her testimony.)

"We have a 9-year-old African American foster son, and whenever we go to church we are confronted by picketers. These confrontations have caused our son to have nightmares and fear church. He always remains on the floor of the car as we go to church. Although we live close enough to church to walk, we don't dare because of the picketers.

"On one occasion, as we were trying to enter the church," [she pauses, near tears] "one of the picketers approached us screaming at our son, 'You're lucky Dr. Eisen didn't abort you!'

"Another time, a protester yelled at my son, 'I can't believe anyone in this church would have a black boy.'" [She sobs after telling this story, then, after a few seconds, she wipes her eyes and continues.]

"No human being can say this is not harmful to children. Please, please remember the Redeemer Lutheran children who ride to church on the floor of their cars and are bullied into using the backdoor to enter church."

SIXTH SPEAKER

Oliver Brooks, 5402 Andover Dr., professor at the university school of law

"This proposed ordinance suffers from a number of defects. For one thing it protects certain groups and targets certain others for restrictions. Also, it fails to leave ample alternative means of expression. The proposal effectively prevents the Regional Rescue picketers from reaching the church members with their message.

"The Supreme Court has upheld a ban on focused picketing around a private home. The court based that ruling on the unique nature of the home. I don't think you can extend that reasoning to a church. In my opinion, that's a quantum leap that cannot be made.

"The columnist Nat Hentoff has said that the power to censor is the strongest urge known to man; sex is a weak second. The speech at issue here is at the very core of the First Amendment. The church members say they want you to protect freedom of religion, but you will not be doing that if you adopt this ordinance. You will be criminalizing one side of a political debate.

"We cannot protect only that speech that is not offensive to small children. If the urge to censor is always with us, the freedoms of speech and religion are always vulnerable.

"The proponents of this ordinance say they want you to protect the children. I ask you, 'What do you want to teach children tonight?' Do you want to teach them that the way to deal with disturbing speech is to pass an ordinance? Or do you want to take a stand for the Bill of Rights?"

Name _____   Class _____   Date _____

SEVENTH SPEAKER
John R. Williams, 814 Harding Ave., director of Regional Rescue

"We've been called everything from bigots to brownshirts to bullies. Now they've added another one: racists.

"We've been accused of terrorism, but the police tell a different story. Undercover police, equipped with surveillance cameras, have never witnessed the actions of which we're accused. How is it all these instances of abuse go undetected virtually under the noses of the police? Are we to believe the police are a bunch of Barney Fifes?

"We reached an agreement with Redeemer Lutheran Church which provided that we would limit the protests with the photographs of aborted babies to the front side of the church. On the back side, we would have a picketer with a sign that has only pictures of babies in the womb. Those who wanted to avoid the pictures of aborted babies could enter by back. Someone might grab the wrong sign, sometimes, but we have tried to adhere to the agreement. If people are disturbed by the pictures and are with kids, why walk by the front of the church? And we don't yell at people going in the church, but we do yell at Dr. Eisen.

"So the question is really whom are you going to believe? Are you going to believe the church members who have a vested interest in criminalizing our actions? Or are you going to believe your police?"

Council Member Roger Lo asked Williams, "Why are you doing this? What would it take to get you to stop?"

"Matthew 18 says if your brother trespasses against you, go first to your brother and confront him. We went to Dr. Eisen, but she is an arrogant, proud abortionist and would not listen. So we went to the church leaders. But the council of Redeemer Lutheran Church did not respond. Instead they made her a council member of their church. When the council members and the ministers refuse to listen, then Matthew 18 says to take it to the whole church. That's what we've been doing. We have gone by scripture. They will have to go by scripture for us to stop. Eisen must repent or be expelled from the church."

EIGHTH SPEAKER
Barry Kopperud, police chief, who was invited by Council Member Luis Ramirez, to speak

"We've had officers at Redeemer Lutheran Church on an occasional basis in response to complaints. We're not there for every event or all the time. Usually we only have one officer present.

"For the past three or four months, we have been present with a group of officers every Sunday. During that time, we've not seen anyone chased; no one's way has been blocked or impeded; no crime has been committed; no terroristic threats have been made."

Council Member Ramirez: "Have you had undercover officers present?"

Kopperud: "Very limited. I've been there in plainclothes about a half dozen times. One other officer has been there occasionally in plainclothes. We also videotaped once. No children were chased on any of these occasions."

NINTH SPEAKER
Jeffry R. Ahson, 49 Groveland Ave, a member of Regional Rescue

"I'm concerned about what I see as a slippery slope. We already have a ban on residential picketing. Now you're considering a ban on church picketing. What's next? Place of business? Social life? Restaurant encounters? It's not your responsibility to make a decision for these two groups, Redeemer Lutheran Church and Regional Rescue, on what is the moral issue of the day.

"It's embarrassing to me as a member of the body of Christ that we're here talking about this. We should be in Redeemer Lutheran Church, two groups of Christians having a discussion over pizza. But I've seen the area around Redeemer Lutheran Church. It's a wealthy neighborhood full of wealthy people who want to get their way. That's what this is all about."

TENTH SPEAKER
Dina Cross, 101 Charow Lane, a member of Regional Rescue

"I'm one of the people who picket Redeemer Lutheran Church. I'm not there every time—at most twice a month. And I always picket at the back entrance to the church. I always hold the sign with the 'nice' picture of the pre-born baby—no aborted or mutilated babies.

"We have explicit instructions not to approach anyone. I don't talk to anyone, unless they talk to me first. I've never witnessed anyone attacking, yelling or abusing the children who go to Redeemer Lutheran Church.

"In fact, on one occasion, a boy—about 11 years old—came up to me and asked me why I was picketing the church and what the sign was about. I explained the whole thing to him, and when I was through, he asked if he could hold the sign with me."

At the end of the hearing, Mayor Sabrina Datolli announced the council would vote on the ordinance at its meeting next week.

Name _____   Class _____   Date _____

EXERCISES TO ACCOMPANY CHAPTER (16)

Brights, Follow-Ups, Roundups, Sidebars and Obituaries

EXERCISE 1: Obituary Leads

INSTRUCTIONS: Write an interesting lead from the following facts. Use your judgment, based on what you have read in this chapter, as to what should be remembered about the person. Correct all errors.

1. Carmen L. DeLaurent, 9, of Spencer, died of head injuries Sunday. She fell in gymnastic practice at the Riordan Studio at 5045 Grant Ave.

    Was the daughter of Steven and Marie DeLaurent.

    Fell while practicing for the Youth Gymnastic State Meet to be held here next month.

    Studied gymnastics since age four at Riordan Studio and hoped to be in the Olympics one day.

    Was a student at Ridgeville Elementary School.

2. William Robert Bailey of Westwood died of heart failure while mowing his lawn at home Thursday. He was 88.

    Graduated from City Industrial College in 1951 with a B.S. degree in business management.

    Was a bombardier in the U.S. Army Air Corps stationed at Harrington, England, in World War II and was shot down by the Germans over Belgium.

    Owner and President of Bailey's Hardware in Westwood.

    Started Bailey's Thanksgiving Table in 1953 to serve 35 hot dinners to people in need. The annual tradition now serves more than 600 dinners at the City Industrial College Auditorium and relies on 75 volunteers.

3. Eva M. Longworth, 37, was a fourth-grade teacher at Central Elementary School in Middlebrook. She died of non-Hodgkin's lymphoma on Monday in Mercy Hospital.

    Was among the first group of patients to receive a bone marrow transplant at Mercy Hospital in Middlebrook 12 years ago.

    Started the cancer survivors' park for teens at Mercy Hospital.

    Accepted a teaching post at Central Elementary School after graduating from Lakeview College in 1991.

4. Ronald (Casey) H. Sikes, 62, of East Landon, a mechanic for T.K. Best Co. gasoline stations, died Saturday.

    Restored 1960s-era Corvette convertibles and owned three—one in red, yellow, and blue.

Name _____   Class _____   Date _____

Graduated from Landon High School in 1963 and worked for Truck & Motor Assembly until it closed in 1987.

Drove one of his Corvettes in the East Landon Labor Day Parade, beginning in 1966.

5. Elizabeth (Liza) Sasso, 20, of Middlebrook, died at Mercy Hospital on Friday after a brief illness. She was the daughter of Catherine and Thomas Sasso.

Was a sophomore at State University.

Loved hiking and exploring rivers and streams.

Joined SU's Environmental Group as a freshman.

Photographed her outdoor excursions and posted them on her website, and advocated against harmful pollutants in regional waterways.

EXERCISE 2: Obituary Notice

INSTRUCTIONS: Write an obituary based on the following information. The first blocks of information are from an obituary form provided by the funeral home. The final block is information you obtained from your reporting.

Full Name of Deceased Kevin Barlow

Age 34

Address 3365 Andover

Date and Cause of Death Cycle accident yesterday

Place of Death In the city—the intersection of Cortez Av. and Alton Rd.

Time and Date of Funeral 2 p.m. Saturday afternoon with visitation at the funeral home from 7-9pm Friday evening and 10–12 noon Saturday

Place of Funeral Woodlawn Funeral Home

Place of Burial Body donated for transplants, with remains to be cremated & scattered.

Officiating Cleric Friends and fellow members of the Resurrection Life Center

Place of Birth Regional Medical Center in this city

Places and Length of Residences Mr. Barlow was a native of the city, attending Hawthorn elementary school and Kennedy high school then served 3 years in the marines. He attended college a year, didn't like it, and joined the police dept. 11 years ago.

Occupation City police officer

Did Deceased Ever Hold Public Office (When and What)? Elected Secretary, then Vice President, and was currently serving in the latter position of the local Police Officer's Benevolent Assn.

Name, Address of Surviving Spouse See below

Maiden Name (if Married Woman) _____

Marriage, When and to Whom See below

Names, Addresses of Surviving Children No children

Five years ago Mr. Barlow celebrated an "Eternal Commitment" ceremony at the Resurrection Life Center with Seth Bernaiche with whom he shared his home.

Name _____   Class _____   Date _____

Names, Addresses of Surviving Brothers and Sisters <u>3 older sisters.</u>
<u>Molly Palomino, 374 Douglass Rd. Jennifer Haself, 544 Beloit Rd. Dorothy</u>
<u>Moravchek, 1487 14th St.</u>

Number of Grandchildren (Great, etc.) <u>None</u>

Names, Addresses of Parents (if Living) <u>Stephen and Harriot Barlow, retired to Fort</u>
<u>Lauderdale, Florida</u>

Other Information <u>3 years ago Mr. Barlow was named the police dept.'s "Officer of</u>
<u>the Year". He was 2nd runnerup in the competition for the states "Officer of the Year"</u>
<u>since that year he pulled a woman and her 4 children from a badly burning house he</u>
<u>spotted while on routine patrol, saving their lives while himself receiving some pain-</u>
<u>ful 2nd and 3rd degree burns. For his action he received the dept's "Medal of Valor," its</u>
<u>highest decoration. He was a member of the dept's Emergency Response Team and was</u>
<u>also a Training Field Officer. He loved motorcycles and, while riding with friends yes-</u>
<u>terday, was hit by an apparently drunk driver who went through a stop sign. He idolized</u>
<u>his grandfather, a policeman in the city, served as an MP in the marines, then returned</u>
<u>to the city to become a police officer. Raised a Catholic, he left to join the Resurrection</u>
<u>Life Center.</u>

Reporter's Additional Notes—Interviews with Friends, Relatives and Co-Workers:

His sister Dorothy said, "It made perfect sense for him to become a police officer. When
he was growing up he always like to see things done right. He expected everyone to do
the right thing. He saw his job as a way of helping the community—putting the bad guys
away, keeping the streets safe for children, mothers, and the good guys."

His mother said, "He was big, 6 feet 4 and 200 pounds, He always liked lifting weights
and working out. He lived with us before we retired to Florida, and he'd come home
with his uniform all torn and dirty after chasing someone. It scared me, but he always
laughed and said there wasn't anyone who could get away from him. He liked tackling.
To him it was a game, like when he played football in high school."

Chief Barry Koperud said, "Officer Barlow was very committed to the community.
All in all, he was an excellent officer. A better person you'll never meet."

His partner Manual Cortez said, "It was hard for Kevin, especially at first, being a gay
cop. He never tried to hide it, and some officers, even today, gave him a hard time, were
real asses about it. But most of us admired him, his courage and all. When you needed
help Kevin was always the first one there, always."

EXERCISE 3: **Writing Obituaries**

INSTRUCTIONS: Write obituaries based on the information given below. Use your judgment, based on
what you have read in this chapter, in deciding whether to use the most controversial details. Be sure to
check facts in the City Directory.

OBITUARY 1: CATHY VERNEL

Identification: Cathy S. Vernel. Born in July 29, 1963. Address: 1010 Vermont St.

Circumstances of death: Died at 4 p.m. today in Roosevelt Hospital. Vernel was admitted to the hospital almost three weeks ago and very slowly died from the AIDS virus.

Funeral services: A memorial service at All Faiths Church will be held at 4 p.m. Saturday. Burial immediately following at Clover Field Cemetery. There will be no viewing of the body. The family will receive visitors Friday from 5 p.m. to 7 p.m. They request no flowers and that expressions of sympathy be in the form of contributions to All Faiths Church.

Survivors: an ex-husband from years ago, Joe Simmons of Hawaii; an adopted daughter, Raynelle of this city; parents, Barbara and Paul Wyman of this city; lots of nieces and nephews.

Accomplishments: Born and attended elementary and high schools in this city. Was graduated with honors from State University with a degree in accounting about 20 years ago. Worked as an accountant for IBM in Chicago for about 15 years, the last five as a senior accountant, and the last two as head of the department.

Additional Information: Quit accounting to become a cab driver in this city. Bought a horse farm. Got into debt and had to sell some of the horses. Was trying to save money to open a horse riding business for little kids. This was something she had always wanted to do.

OBITUARY 2: JOEL FOULER

Identification: Joel Fritz Fouler. Born March 13, 1984. Address: 2006 Hillcrest St.

Circumstances of death: Taken to the emergency room at Mercy Hospital at 1 a.m. yesterday, where he died shortly thereafter. An autopsy will be conducted because police found some drugs in his residence, which he shared with another student.

Funeral services: The family will see people at Safe Haven Funeral home from 2 to 4 p.m. tomorrow and the funeral follows at 5 p.m. Burial immediately following at Glenn Acres Cemetery. Donations can be made to the school for a scholarship in Fouler's name.

Survivors: His parents, Barbara and Fritz of 88 Eastbrook Avenue.

Three sisters, Wendy, Sierra and Regina, all at home. A brother, Frederic, a soldier stationed in Germany. Also, his college roommate of the last two years: Timothy Bolankner, also of 2006 Hillcrest St..

Accomplishments: In the top 10 percent of his graduating class at Central High School, where he was a member of the baseball, basketball and soccer teams, a member of the student council, a member of the National Honor Society. Now, a sophomore studying veterinerary medicine in hopes of becoming a veterinarian someday. He maintained a 3.8 gpa in college and was on the Dean's List. He was also on the baseball team.

EXERCISE 4: Roundups

Roundups—Multiple Events

INSTRUCTIONS: Write a single roundup story that summarizes all three of the fires described below. Correct all errors.

Name _____   **Class** _____   **Date** _____

FIRE 1

Two police officers patrolling Main St. reported a fire at Frishe's Bowling Alley, 4113 Main St., at 3:32 a.m. today. They smelled smoke, got out of their squad car and traced the smoke to the bowling alley. Firefighters said the fire was confined to an office, where it caused an estimated $10,000 in damage. Firefighters found evidence of arson and notified police that the office apparently had been set on fire after it was burglarized. Two cigarette machines, a soft-drink machine and a door leading to the office had been pried open. Police said the thieves probably set the fire to hide the robbery. Art Mahew, manager of the bowling alley, estimated that $20 was missing from the three machines and $50 was taken from a cash box in the office. He added: "That's all the money we keep in the building at night. Except for some change for the next day's business, we just don't keep any money in the building at night. It's too risky. This is the third robbery we've had since I started working here four years ago."

FIRE 2

Firefighters were called to 1314 Griese Drive at 8:23 a.m. today. They found a fire in progress on the second floor of the two-story home. The home is owned by Mr. and Mrs. Timothy Keele. Mr. and Mrs. Keel and their four children escaped from the home before firemen arrived. Firefighters extinguished the blaze within 20 minutes. The fire was confined to two upstairs bedrooms and the attic. Smoke and water damage were reported throughout the house. No one was injured. Damage was estimated at $20,000. Mrs. Keel told firemen she had punished one of her children for playing with matches in an upstairs closet earlier in the morning. Fire marshals said the blaze started in that closet and attributed the fire to the child playing with matches. Mrs. Keel added that she was not aware of the fire until a telephone repairman working across the street noticed smoke, came over and rang her doorbell. When she answered, he asked, "Do you know your house is on fire?"

FIRE 3

Firefighters responded to a call at the Quality Trailer Court at 10:31 a.m. today after neighbors were alerted by screams from a trailer occupied by Mrs. Susan Kopp, age 71. Flames had spread throughout the trailer by the time firefighters arrived at the scene. The firefighters had to extinguish the blaze, then wait for the embers to cool before they were able to enter the trailer. They found Mrs. Kopp's body in her bedroom in the trailer. A spokesman for the Fire Department said she had apparently been smoking in bed, then awoke when her bedding caught fire. She died of suffocation before she could get out. Neighbors who heard her screams were unable to enter the trailer because of the flames, smoke and heat.

EXERCISE 5: Brights

INSTRUCTIONS: Use the following information to write "brights," a series of short, humorous stories. Write some brights that have a summary lead and others that have a surprise ending.

1. BANK REGULATIONS

Abraham Burmeister is president of the First National Bank, the largest bank in your community. Each year, in accordance with new federal laws, the bank is required to send all its customers copies of some complex new federal rules concerning the regulation of banks and the procedures followed for money transfers by means of electronic banking. Consequently, the First National Bank prepared a 4,500-word pamphlet describing and summarizing those new federal rules and then sent copies of the rules to all its 40,000 regular depositors and customers. Like many other bankers, Burmeister objected to the federal law, saying it imposed a needless burden and needless expense on bankers since the federal laws that banks are being forced to explain are too complicated for the average person to understand and too dull and uninteresting for people to spend time trying to read. To prove his point, on the last page of 100 of the 40,000 copies of the rules he took a gamble and inserted a special extra sentence. The sentence said, "If you return this pamphlet to any of the banks tellers within the next 30 days, they will give you $50." The 30 days passed yesterday and not one person turned in a single copy of the 100 special pamphlets and requested the $50 due on demand, apparently because no one read the pamphlets. Bank officials calculated that it cost somewhere in the neighborhood of $25,000 to prepare, print, address and mail the pamphlets to the 40,000 bank customers, and they said that is a waste of money, yet they must do it every year, even though obviously no one reads the things, as they have just proven with their interesting little experiment.

2. DRUNKEN RIDER

Lynita L. Sharp admits she was intoxicated last night but says she should not be charged with drunk driving. Sharp, 5836 Bolling Dr., was riding her 2-year-old filly horse along a state highway when Scott Forsyth, a corporal in the sheriff's department, came along. Forsyth said he saw Sharp sitting on her horse in the middle of the road. He said the rider looked to be sick or asleep. He turned on the blue lights on his cruiser, and the horse bolted off. Sharp said she was spending the weekend with her friends who own the farm where her horse is stabled. She had spent part of the evening at the local tavern and was riding home. Sharp said the cruisers light spooked the horse and caused her to lose control of it. Forsythe issued Sharp a ticket for operating a vehicle while under the influence of an intoxicating substance. Sharp said her horse, Frosty, is not a vehicle. "Vehicles can't think, but Frosty can think for herself," Sharp said. "I've fallen asleep in the saddle before, but it doesn't matter because Frosty knows the way home." Donald Hendricks, the assistant county attorney, said the state law does not require that a person be operating a motorized vehicle in order to be cited for drunk driving. The law was changed in 1991, he said, and since then 23 people who were not operating motorized vehicles, including a bicyclist and a man in a wheelchair, have been arrested for driving while intoxicated.

EXERCISES TO ACCOMPANY CHAPTER (17)

Public Affairs Reporting

EXERCISE 1: Public Affairs Reporting

911 Emergency: The Dahmer Tapes

Police officers in Milwaukee, Wisconsin, found 11 mutilated bodies in an apartment rented by Jeffrey L. Dahmer. Dahmer, 31, confessed to killing a total of 17 people and pleaded that he was insane. One of Dahmer's victims was a 14-year-old Laotian boy, Konerak Sinthasomphone, whom the police might have saved. When he was finally arrested, Dahmer told police that two officers had been at his apartment two months earlier to investigate a 911 call involving the 14-year-old. The officers left the boy at the apartment, and Dahmer then killed him.

The police later released this transcript of the 911 call. It reveals that a Milwaukee resident named Glenda Cleveland called the police at 2 a.m. the previous May 27. Cleveland told a 911 dispatcher that her daughter and a niece had seen the boy naked on a street corner and that the boy needed help. In a follow-up call, Cleveland, 37, asked the officers if they were certain that the boy was an adult.

A week before the tape's release, the two officers were suspended with pay but not identified. A lawyer representing the officers said they had seen no evidence at Dahmer's apartment to suggest that anything was wrong. Also, they believed that the naked male was a man living with Dahmer. The officers' lawyer added that they tried to interview the boy but that he seemed to be seriously intoxicated.

INSTRUCTIONS: Assume that the Milwaukee police (1) have already found the bodies and interviewed Dahmer, (2) suspended the officers one week ago and (3) released the transcript today. Write a news story that summarizes the transcript's content. Because this is a verbatim copy of the transcript, you can quote it directly. Include whatever background information seems necessary.

DISPATCHER:	"Milwaukee emergency. Operator 71."
WOMAN:	"OK. Hi. I am on 25th and State. And there's this young man. He's butt-naked and he has been beaten up. He is very bruised up. He can't stand. He is . . . butt-naked. He has no clothes on. He is really hurt. And I, you know, ain't got no coat on. But I just seen him. He needs some help."
DISPATCHER:	"Where is he at?"
WOMAN:	"25th and State. The corner of 25th and State."
DISPATCHER:	"He's just on the corner of the street?"
WOMAN:	"He's in the middle of the street. He (unintelligible). We tried to help him. Some people trying to help him."
DISPATCHER:	"OK. And he's unconscious right now?"
WOMAN:	"He is getting him up. 'Cause he is bruised up. Somebody must have jumped on him and stripped him or whatever."
DISPATCHER:	"OK. Let me put the fire department on the line. They will send an ambulance. Just stay on the phone. OK?"
WOMAN:	"OK."

Name _____   Class _____   Date _____

	[The dispatcher transferred the call to the fire department, and the woman asked for an ambulance, saying a "butt-naked young boy or man or whatever" needed help.]
WOMAN:	"He's been beaten up real bad. . . . He can't stand up. . . . He has no clothes on. He is very hurt."
FIRE DEPARTMENT DISPATCHER:	"Is he awake?"
WOMAN:	"He ain't awake. They are trying to get him to walk, but he can't walk straight. He can't even see straight. Any time he stands up he just falls down."
DISPATCHER:	"25th and State? All right. OK."
	[The woman hung up. The next part of the tape is a police radio transmission of a dispatcher reporting the woman's call to a street officer.]
DISPATCHER:	"36. I got a man down. Caller states there is a man badly beaten and is wearing no clothes, lying in the street, 2-5 and State. Anonymous female caller. Ambulance sent."
OFFICER:	"10-4."
	[A Milwaukee emergency operator received information from the sheriff's department, checking on another call that reported a male dragging a naked male who looked injured.]
EMERGENCY OPERATOR:	"OK. We will get someone out."
	[The next conversation involved an officer reporting back to the dispatcher over the police radio.]
OFFICER:	"36. . . . Intoxicated Asian, naked male. (Laughter.) Was returned to his sober boyfriend. (More laughter.)"
	[An officer advised (C-10) that the assignment was completed (C-18) and the squad was ready for new duties (10-8). There was a 40-second gap in the tape, then:]
OFFICER:	"Squad 65."
DISPATCHER:	"65."
OFFICER:	"Ah, give myself and 64 C-10 and put us 10-8."
DISPATCHER:	"10-4 64 and 65."
OFFICER:	"10-4. It will be a minute. My partner is going to get deloused at the station. (Laughter.)"
DISPATCHER:	"10-4."
	[A woman later called Milwaukee Emergency and told the dispatcher that 10 minutes ago her daughter and niece "flagged down" a policeman after they "walked up on a young child being molested by a male guy." She said the officers took no information from the girls, and the boy was naked and bleeding. The woman said further information "must be needed." The dispatcher asked the location of the incident, and the woman repeated that her daughter's and niece's names were not taken.]
WOMAN:	"The fact is a crime was being committed. I am sure you must need, you know, some kind of information based on that."
	[The call was transferred, and the woman repeated the squad number and the address of the incident. The woman asked if squad car 68 "brought someone in, a child being molested by an adult that was witnessed by my daughter and niece."]

Name _____   **Class** _____   **Date** _____

WOMAN:	"Their names or nothing was taken down and I wonder if this situation was being handled.... What it indicated was that this was a male child being raped and molested by an adult."
	[The police agent referred the call to another district after getting the address of the incident. The woman repeated her story again to another official. Eventually, she reached an officer who was at the scene.]
OFFICER:	"Hello. This is . . . of the Milwaukee Police."
WOMAN:	"Yes. There was a squad car number 68 that was flagged down earlier this evening. About 15 minutes ago."
OFFICER:	"That was me."
WOMAN:	"Ya, ah, what happened? I mean my daughter and my niece witnessed what was going on. Was anything done about the situation? Do you need their names or information or anything from them?"
OFFICER:	"No, not at all."
WOMAN:	"You don't?"
OFFICER:	"Nope. It's an intoxicated boyfriend of another boyfriend."
WOMAN:	"Well, how old was this child?"
OFFICER:	"It wasn't a child, it was an adult."
WOMAN:	"Are you sure?"
OFFICER:	"Yup."
WOMAN:	"Are you positive? Because this child doesn't even speak English. My daughter had, you know, dealt with him before, seeing him on the street."
OFFICER:	"Hmmm. Yea. No. He's, he's, oh, it's all taken care of, ma'am."
WOMAN:	"Are you sure?"
OFFICER:	"Ma'am. I can't make it any more clear. It's all taken care of. That's, you know, he's with his boyfriend and, ah, his boyfriend's apartment, where he's got his belongings also. And that is where it is released."
WOMAN:	"Isn't this, I mean, what if he's a child and not an adult. I mean are you positive this is an adult?"
OFFICER:	"Ma'am. Ma'am. Like I explained to you. It is all taken care of. It's as positive as I can be. OK. I can't do anything about somebody's sexual preferences in life."
WOMAN:	"Well, no, I am not saying anything about that, but it appeared to have been a child. This is my concern."
OFFICER:	"No. No. He's not."
WOMAN:	"He's not a child?"
OFFICER:	"No, he's not. OK? And it's a boyfriend–boyfriend thing. And he's got belongings at the house where he came from."
WOMAN:	"Hmmmm. Hmmm."
OFFICER:	"He has got very . . . pictures of himself and his boyfriend and so forth. So. . . ."
WOMAN:	"Oh, I see."
OFFICER:	"OK."
WOMAN:	"OK. I am just, you know, it appeared to have been a child. That was my concern."
OFFICER:	"I understand. No, he is not. Nope."
WOMAN:	"Oh. OK. Thank you. 'Bye."

Name _____ Class _____ Date _____

EXERCISE 2: Public Affairs Reporting

School District Budget

INSTRUCTIONS: Write a news story summarizing the statement from the superintendent of schools and the proposed school district budget that follows. The statement appears verbatim and may be quoted directly. Accompanying the budget are figures showing enrollment by grade and the number of people the district employs. As you write your story, you might want to use a calculator (or a computer spreadsheet program) to find some numbers the budget does not provide, such as the percentage by which spending will increase or the average annual salary for teachers.

STATEMENT ON THE PROPOSED BUDGET
By Gary Hubbard
Superintendent of Schools

The development of this budget for the coming year was a challenging process. The district staff had only one overriding premise: What educational programs will provide every student with the opportunity to reach his or her fullest potential and provide the community with contributing citizens? This is an important goal because if this community is to continue to grow, prosper and maintain its quality of life, we must have educated citizens. This community historically has committed itself to maintaining the quality of the school system, and we are sure it will continue to do so.

This budget proposal shows what the district staff thinks is necessary to maintain the quality of schools and is based on certain assumptions which should be made public:

1. We expect growth in the district's assessed valuation of 28% next year. The county assessor will not certify the final assessed valuation for the district until after the deadline for adopting this budget.

2. The Legislature changed the formula by which state aid is distributed. The impact of that change is not clear, but we expect that state aid will increase only slightly for the next year, but more substantial increases of $700,000 to $1 million may be coming in the two or three years after next.

3. Student spending will remain at about $3,000 per pupil, and the district's enrollment will grow modestly.

4. The ratio of teachers to students will remain constant.

5. No new programs will be started.

6. No programs will be restarted.

7. Salaries and fringe benefits will not increase, but spending on nonsalary items will increase 2.5% in accordance with the consumer price index.

The General Fund Budget shows the staff's proposals for expenditures for most of the district's day-to-day operations, including all instructional programs. All expenses for operating the district's three high schools, nine middle schools and thirty-three elementary schools are in the general fund. It also includes all salaries for administrators, certified teachers and classified non-teaching employees.

The Building and Construction Budget shows spending on the construction of three new elementary schools and the work being done to renovate and remodel two middle schools. The district is nearing completion of the building program voters approved five years ago when they passed a $54-million bond issue. Some of the construction and renovation work that had been budgeted for this year was delayed because of bad weather. Therefore, money the district had expected to spend last year has been included in this year's budget.

The Interscholastic Athletics Fund Budget covers expenditures on interscholastic sports, such as football, girls' volleyball, girls' and boys' basketball, boys' baseball and girls' softball. Salaries for full-time coaches come from the General Fund. The salaries paid from the Interscholastic Athletics Fund go to referees, parking attendants, concessions workers and security personnel.

The Debt Service Fund shows district payments on the principal and interest for the various bond issues outstanding.

DEFINITIONS OF BUDGET CATEGORIES:

Salaries—Funds paid to employees under regular employment contracts with the district.

Benefits—Funds for the district's share of Social Security, retirement, unemployment benefits, health insurance and death benefits.

Contracted Services—Funds to pay for services provided by individuals or firms outside the district. Examples are attorneys' fees, consultant fees and maintenance agreements on equipment.

Supplies—Funds for consumable materials used in providing district services, such as textbooks, pencils, chalk, paper, floor wax, gasoline, etc.

Instructional Development—Funds allocated to improve instructional programs and for professional growth activities by employees.

In-District Travel—Funds paid to reimburse district employees who are required by their job assignments to travel within the district.

Repair Equipment—Funds allocated to repair equipment such as typewriters, film projectors, lighting fixtures and musical instruments.

Replace/New Equipment—Funds for the purchase of equipment to provide new services or enhance current programs. Examples are microcomputers, copying machines, vehicles, tools and furniture.

Fixed Charges—Funds allocated to purchase various kinds of insurance for the district.

Transfer—Funds transferred from the General Fund to support athletics, debate, journalism and other student activities.

Contingency—Funds budgeted for unexpected personnel and non-personnel items and which can be expended only with board approval.

Name _____   Class _____   Date _____

SCHOOL DISTRICT BUDGET

DESCRIPTION	LAST YEAR ACTUAL	THIS YEAR BUDGET	NEXT YEAR PROPOSED
GENERAL FUND			
Beg. Balance 9/1	14,727,807.00	17,552,056.00	14,174,366.00
Receipts			
Property Taxes	91,798,484.00	91,485,010.00	102,793,572.00
State Aid	29,236,428.00	31,373,050.00	31,427,590.00
Other Local	5,785,741.00	5,847,000.00	5,971,000.00
County	857,522.00	1,000,000.00	841,000.00
State	18,744,139.00	21,566,000.00	21,451,000.00
Federal	2,950,850.00	3,457,000.00	3,625,000.00
Total Receipts	149,373,164.00	154,728,060.00	166,109,162.00
Total Revenue Available	164,101,335.00	172,298,116.00	180,283,528.00
Property Tax Rate	1.5571	1.6453	1.4126
Valuation	5,572,804,000.00	5,702,528,000.00	7,301,758,000.00
Expenditures			
Personnel Expenses			
Salaries			
Administration	7,924,457.00	8,320,440.00	8,447,610.00
Certificated	76,144,423.00	80,556,450.00	87,034,960.00
Classified	19,413,780.00	21,297,550.00	21,982,000.00
Total Salaries	103,482,660.00	110,174,440.00	117,464,570.00
Benefits	26,117,570.00	29,405,560.00	30,723,020.00
Total Personnel Expenses	129,600,230.00	139,580,000.00	148,187,590.00
Non-Personnel Expenses			
Contract Services	1,716,125.00	2,588,010.00	2,570,590.00
Supplies	6,685,297.00	7,586,510.00	7,650,980.00
Utilities	3,081,556.00	3,036,980.00	3,566,700.00
Professional Development	386,739.00	384,430.00	391,930.00
In-District Travel	171,513.00	163,900.00	163,750.00
Repair Equipment	265,977.00	317,430.00	317,930.00
Replace/New Equipment	2,738,604.00	3,093,640.00	3,147,250.00
Fixed Charges	1,507,858.00	1,409,200.00	1,447,400.00
Transfers	395,380.00	363,650.00	348,150.00
Total Non-Personnel Expenses	16,949,049.00	18,943,750.00	19,604,680.00
Total Expenses	146,549,279.00	158,523,750.00	167,792,270.00
Contingency	0.00	100,000.00	0.00
Grand Total Expenses	146,549,279.00	158,623,750.00	167,792,270.00
Ending Fund Balance	17,552,056.00	13,674,366.00	12,491,258.00

Name _____   **Class** _____   **Date** _____

DESCRIPTION	LAST YEAR ACTUAL	THIS YEAR BUDGET	NEXT YEAR PROPOSED
BUILDING AND CONSTRUCTION FUND			
Beginning Balance 9/1	3,383,807.00	54,536,777.00	46,633,343.00
Receipts			
Property Taxes	8,206,489.00	7,895,636.00	6,419,926.00
In Lieu of Taxes	241,790.00	260,000.00	260,000.00
Interest on Investments	97,280.00	1,550,000.00	1,730,000.00
Land Leases	5,024.00	10,000.00	5,000.00
City Reimbursements	510,898.00	580,000.00	75,000.00
Miscellaneous	42,394.00	50,000.00	50,000.00
Roof Replacement Fund	0.00	1,000,000.00	900,000.00
Motor Vehicle Taxes	28,578.00	20,000.00	20,000.00
Bond Proceeds	53,705,054.00	0.00	0.00
Tax Anticipation	0.00	5,828,700.00	3,198,344.00
Total Receipts	62,837,507.00	17,194,336.00	12,658,270.00
Total Available	66,221,314.00	71,731,113.00	59,291,613.00
Expenditures			
Construction	8,535,662.00	29,923,852.00	55,390,460.00
Renovation	2,933,242.00	1,150,000.00	1,000,000.00
Connectivity	0.00	0.00	1,225,000.00
Roof Replacement	0.00	1,000,000.00	959,153.00
Purchase of Sites	7,883.00	0.00	0.00
Tax Collection Fee	75,892.00	80,000.00	82,000.00
Rating and Management Fees	131,858.00	0.00	0.00
Contingency	0.00	500,000.00	0.00
Not Completed Projects	0.00	3,545,348.00	1,000,000.00
Principal/Interest Accrual	0.00	0.00	335,000.00
Total Expenditures	11,684,537.00	36,199,200.00	59,991,613.00
Ending Balance	54,536,777.00	35,531,913.00	0.00
DEBT SERVICES FUND BUDGET			
Beginning Balance 9/1	799,305.00	8,689,915.00	1,342,124.00
Receipts			
Property Tax	2,305,785.00	7,075,000.00	7,442,500.00
In Lieu of Tax	61,198.00	100,000.00	100,000.00
Motor Vehicle Taxes	7,578.00	10,000.00	10,000.00
Interest	159,196.00	218,660.00	100,000.00
Refunding	7,945,815.00	0.00	0.00
Total Receipts	10,479,572.00	7,403,660.00	7,652,500.00
Total Available	11,278,877.00	16,093,575.00	8,994,624.00

continued

Name _____   Class _____   Date _____

DESCRIPTION	LAST YEAR ACTUAL	THIS YEAR BUDGET	NEXT YEAR PROPOSED
Expenditures			
Bond Principal			
4,280,000 Issued six years ago	325,000.00	3,225,000.00	0.00
5,000,000 Issued five years ago	345,000.00	4,005,000.00	0.00
3,500,000 Issued four years ago	240,000.00	380,000.00	415,000.00
4,220,000 Issued three years ago	110,000.00	180,000.00	190,000.00
8,020,000 Refunding two years ago	430,000.00	1,255,000.00	1,285,000.00
54,480,000 Issued last year	0.00	475,000.00	1,475,000.00
Total Principal	1,450,000.00	9,520,000.00	3,365,000.00
Bond Interest	1,091,477.00	6,096,168.00	5,529,489.00
Tax Collection Fee	21,455.00	70,000.00	70,000.00
Management Fees	26,030.00	33,241.00	30,135.00
Total Expenditures	2,588,962.00	15,719,409.00	8,994,624.00
Ending Balance	8,689,915.00	374,166.00	0.00
INTERSCHOLASTIC ATHLETICS FUND BUDGET			
Beginning Balance 9/1	71,272.00	72,303.00	72,229.00
Receipts			
Football	125,036.00	75,000.00	75,000.00
Basketball (Boys')	48,922.00	40,000.00	50,000.00
Basketball (Girls')	24,794.00	25,000.00	25,000.00
Other	104,148.00	100,000.00	100,160.00
Transferred from General Fund	294,120.00	238,390.00	228,230.00
Total Receipts	597,020.00	478,390.00	478,390.00
Total Available	668,292.00	550,693.00	550,619.00
Expenditures			
Salaries, supplies, equipment	595,989.00	505,964.00	505,964.00
Total Expenditures	595,989.00	505,964.00	505,964.00
Ending Balance	72,303.00	44,729.00	44,655.00
SUMMARY OF ALL FUNDS			
Total Available Revenues	242,269,818.00	260,673,497.00	249,120,384.00
Total Expenditures	161,418,767.00	211,048,323.00	237,284,471.00
Ending Balance	80,851,051.00	49,625,174.00	11,835,913.00

Name _____   Class _____   Date _____

DISTRICT ENROLLMENT

GRADE	LAST YEAR	THIS YEAR	NEXT YEAR
Kindergarten	2,348	2,193	2,349
1st	2,367	2,347	2,225
2nd	2,378	2,377	2,347
3rd	2,415	2,371	2,373
4th	2,421	2,406	2,386
5th	2,326	2,424	2,398
6th	2,322	2,319	2,435
7th	2,292	2,367	2,302
8th	2,071	2,289	2,335
9th	2,118	2,082	2,265
10th	2,078	2,141	2,112
11th	1,969	2,015	2,089
12th	2,070	2,057	2,006
Special Education	296	367	367
Head Start	267	265	265
Total	29,738	30,020	30,254

DISTRICT EMPLOYMENT (FULL-TIME EQUIVALENCY)

CATEGORY	LAST YEAR	THIS YEAR	NEXT YEAR
Administration	127.95	131.30	132.30
Certificated	2,225.63	2,313.38	2,369.26
Technician	62.00	65.70	136.14
Office Personnel	270.60	274.55	263.05
Paraeducators	574.74	599.97	549.54
Tradespersons	435.13	467.50	467.55
Total	3,696.05	3,852.40	3,917.84

EXPLANATION OF CODES FOR TRAFFIC ACCIDENT REPORT
(To Accompany Exercise 3 in Textbook)

Vehicle damage area

- 01-Front
- 02-Passenger side front
- 03-Passenger side
- 04-Passenger side rear
- 05-Rear
- 06-Driver side rear
- 07-Driver side
- 08-Driver side front

Damage scale

Rate from 1–5 with 1 being no visible damage and 5 being extensive damage.

Damage severity

Rate from 1–5 with 1 being little or no damage and 5 being inoperable and unrepairable.

Safety equipment (on vehicle)

- 01-No lap belts, shoulder belts or airbag
- 02-Lap belts only
- 03-Lap & shoulder belts only
- 04-Airbags, driver's side only
- 05-Airbags, driver and passenger
- 06-Airbags, front and side
- 07-Other
- 08-Unknown

Race

- C-Caucasian
- N-Negro
- A-Asian
- U-Unknown

Sex

- M-Male
- F-Female

Name _____ **Class** _____ **Date** _____

Safety E. (Safety equipment used)

01-None used
02-Lap & shoulder belt used
03-Shoulder belt only used
04-Lap belt only used
05-Airbag deployed
06-Airbag not deployed
07-Airbag not available
08-Child safety seat used
09-Child booster seat used
10-Helmet used
11-Restraint use unknown

Eject. (Ejected/Trapped)

01-Not ejected or trapped
02-Partially ejected
03-Totally ejected
04-Trapped; occupant removed without equipment
05-Trapped; equipment used in extrication
06-Unknown

Injury (Injury severity)

01-Killed
02-Disabled; cannot leave
scene without assistance (broken bones, severe cuts, prolonged unconsciousness, etc.)
03-Visible but not disabling (minor cuts, swelling, etc.)
04-Possible but not visible (complaint of pain, etc.)
05-None

Drivers and Vehicles (indicate all that may apply)

Physical defects prior to accident

01-Apparently normal
02-Eyesight impaired, wearing corrective lenses
03-Eyesight impaired, not wearing corrective lenses
04-Impairment to hands or arms

05-Impairment to feet or legs

06-Impairment to hands/arms and feet/legs

Vehicle defects prior to accident

01-None

02-Broken or inoperable headlights

03-Broken or inoperable tail lights

04-Broken or inoperable turn signals

05-Cracked or damaged windshield

06-Cracked or damage side or rear windows

07-Insufficient tread on tires

08-Malfunctioning brakes

09-Malfunctioning steering

10-Other

11-Unknown

Contributing circumstances

01-No improper driving

02-Failed to yield right of way

03-Disregarded traffic signs, signals, road markings

04-Exceeded authorized speed limit

05-Driving too fast for conditions

06-Made improper turn

07-Wrong side or wrong way

08-Followed too closely

09-Failed to keep in proper lane or ran off road

10-Operating vehicle in erratic, negligent, reckless, careless or aggressive manner

11-Swerved due to wind, slippery surface, other object or pedestrian

12-Over-correcting/oversteering

13-Visibility obstructed

14-Inattention

15-Mobile phone distraction

16-Distracted-other

17-Fatigued/asleep

18-Operating defective equipment

19-Other improper action

20-Unknown

Name _____   **Class** _____   **Date** _____

Lighting condition

    01-Daylight

    02-Dawn

    03-Dusk

    04-Dark; lighted roadway

    05-Dark; roadway not lighted

    06-Dark; unknown roadway lighting

    07-Other

    08-Unknown

Weather

    01-Fair

    02-Cloudy

    03-Fog, smog, smoke

    04-Rain

    05-Sleet, hail, freezing rain/drizzle

    06-Snow

    07-Severe crosswinds

    08-Blowing sand, soil, dirt, snow

    09-Other

    10-Unknown

Road surface

    01-Concrete

    02-Asphalt

    03-Brick

    04-Gravel

    05-Dirt

    06-Other

Road defects

    01-None

    02-Oil, sand or gravel on surface

    03-Ruts, holes, bumps

    04-Construction zone

    05-Worn, polished surface

    06-Obstruction in road

07-Traffic control device inoperative

09-Shoulders (none, low, soft, high)

Traffic control

01-None

02-Traffic control signal

03-Flashing traffic control signal

04-School zone signal

05-Stop sign

06-Yield sign

07-Warning sign

08-Railroad crossing device

09-Unknown

Type location

01-Intersection (3-way)

02-Intersection (4-way)

03-Public street or highway

04-Private driveway or parking lot

Trafficway character

01-Straight and level

02-Straight and on slope

03-Straight and on hilltop

04-Curved and level

05-Curved and on slope

06-Curved and on hilltop

Trafficway lanes

01-One lane

02-Two lanes

03-Three lanes

04-Four lanes

05-Five lanes

06-Six or more lanes

Name _____   **Class** _____   **Date** _____

Vision obscured

    01-No obstruction

    02-Obstruction in one or more of the vehicles (passengers, cargo, etc.)

    03-Shrubs, trees

    04-Walls, buildings

    05-Roads intersect at odd angle

    06-Other vehicles

Class of trafficway

    01-Residential street

    02-Arterial street

    03-Highway, uncontrolled access

    04-Highway, controlled access

Type of trafficway

    01-Undivided two-way traffic

    02-Two-way traffic separated by yellow line

    03-Two-way traffic separated by median

    04-One way traffic

    05-One-way traffic with two or more lanes

EXERCISES TO ACCOMPANY CHAPTER 18

Introduction to Investigative Reporting

EXERCISE 1: Investigative Journalism

A classmate approaches you because she knows that you work for the student media. She is on the field hockey team, and she tells you that the graduation rate for student–athletes at your college has dropped significantly in the past three years. Budget concerns at the institution resulted in the elimination of all staff in the student–athlete support services office five years ago. What sources—primary and secondary—would you need for the story? What kinds of data would you need to gather to support the facts in the story?

Consider the digital and visual journalistic elements that you would employ in creating a package for the web and social media. What sources would you interview on video or for audio clips? What B-roll would you record? What still photography might you include? How could you use crowd sourcing through social media to gather information for this story? Finally, thinking ethically, what implications or consequences might arise for the college from publication of the story? How do you defend your decision to pursue and publish the story?

Name _____   Class _____   Date _____

Journalism and Public Relations

EXERCISE 1: Evaluating News Releases

INSTRUCTIONS: Critically evaluate the newsworthiness of the following leads. Each lead appeared in a news release mailed to news organizations. Determine whether each release is usable as written and why. Then discuss your decision with your classmates.

1. Pregnant women throughout the state are finding it more difficult to locate an obstetrician willing to deliver their baby because of the number of obstetricians—80 last year alone—who are discontinuing the practice because of the high cost of malpractice insurance, according to a survey by the State Obstetric and Gynecologic Society.

    EVALUATION: _____

2. During October, millions of high school seniors and their families will attend college fairs and tour campuses nationwide as they select a college for next fall. Planning experts at Morris College say that families should not automatically eliminate a college because of its sticker price.

    EVALUATION: _____

3. High interest rates, coupled with low prices for most agricultural commodities, are causing serious "cash-flow" problems for farmers, pushing some toward bankruptcy, according to a study by the Institute of Food and Agricultural Sciences (IFAS) at your state university.

    EVALUATION: _____

4. Nail polish remover is still being dropped into the eyes of conscious rabbits to meet insurance regulations, infant primates are punished by electric shocks in pain endurance tests, and dogs are reduced to a condition called "learned helplessness" to earn someone a PhD.

    With the theme "Alternatives Now," People for the Ethical Treatment of Animals (PETA) is sponsoring a community rally on Friday—World Day for Laboratory Animals—at 1 p.m.

    EVALUATION: _____

5. Until recently, a missing lockbox key could be a major security problem for homeowners selling a house. But today, a missing electronic key can be turned off, protecting clients and their homes. More and more homesellers are using an electronic lockbox, the Superior KeyBox from Williams, on their properties to provide added safety, security and convenience for their homes.

EVALUATION: _____

6. Natural Gardening, the world's largest-circulation gardening magazine, has announced that it has retained Balenti Associates to represent its advertising sales in the Midwest and western United States. The 27-year-old company is one of the largest advertising sales firms in the United States, with sales offices in the top five U.S. markets as well as major European cities.

EVALUATION: _____

7. "The Changing Face of Men's Fashion" will be illustrated in a fashion presentation in Robinson's Men's Shop at 5:30 on Thursday. A special feature of the event will be commentary on the distinctive directions in men's designs by fashion designer Anna Zella.

EVALUATION: _____

8. In cooperation with the U.S. Consumer Product Safety Commission (CPSC), the Moro division of the Petrillo Group of Italy is announcing the recall of 31,000 London branch LP gas Monitor Gauges. Some of these gauges may leak highly flammable propane gas that could ignite or explode. CPSC is aware of five incidents of gas leaks catching fire. Two of these fires resulted in burn injuries.

EVALUATION: _____

9. Dr. Zena Treemont, who recently retired after 35 years with the U.S. Department of Agriculture, has assumed her new duties as Chief of the Bureau of Brucellosis and Tuberculosis with the State Department of Agriculture and Consumer Services, Commissioner Doyle Conner announced today.

EVALUATION: _____

10. Women have made much progress against discrimination through social and legal reforms, but they are still the victims of a very disabling form of discrimination that largely goes unnoticed: arthritis.
    Of the more than 31 million Americans who suffer from arthritis, two-thirds are women, according to the Arthritis Foundation.

EVALUATION: _____

Name _____ Class _____ Date _____

EXERCISE 2: **Writing News Releases**

INSTRUCTIONS: The following information is from an actual news release. Write a news release from the information provided. Remember to use Associated Press style. Use as much information as you think necessary to create an effective release. Add phrases and transitions to make the news release acceptable to editors. List yourself as the contact person for the sponsor of the release, decide on the release date and write a headline.

NEWS RELEASE
FROM: MADISON PANCAKE FESTIVAL
     P.O. Box 5029
     Madison

MADISON PANCAKE FESTIVAL

MADISON'S Seventeenth Annual Pancake Festival takes place this Saturday and Sunday.

The Festival has always been non-profit, sponsored by the Betterment Association of the Madison Area, Inc. and for the past three years, has been co-sponsored with the Madison Area Jaycees.

Civic organizations, churches, school children, City Hall employees, inmates from the Copeland Road Prison, local businesses and residents from surrounding areas all work together to stage a smooth-running two-day event that over the past 16 years has drawn almost a million people to this small town of 3,200.

From last year's proceeds, money was donated to the city of Madison to be used for park improvements. Monies also were donated to the Madison Volunteer Fire Department and the Gateway Ambulance Service. Also a portion of the proceeds were set aside for scholarships for local high school students.

The volunteers' successful efforts to stage the Festival show what communities can do on their own—with ingenuity, determination, and effort. *Nobody gets paid. All work is volunteer.* Chief lure of the Festival is the picturesque and historic town itself.

The menu consists of pancakes with your choice of delectable toppings such as nuts, berries (blueberries, raspberries or strawberries), jams, syrups, bananas, and much, much more. These Pancake Plates will be served both days, from 7 AM to 9 PM on Saturday and Sunday. A Pancake Plate will cost $12 for adults and $6 for children 12 and under. That one low price includes the cost of admission to the festival and free refills for an entire day.

Visitors will also be able to purchase tickets for a drawing on a 16-foot boat, a trailer, and a 45 HP outboard motor sponsored by the Madison Volunteer Fire Dept.

There will be over 100 booths to display a large selection of the finest arts and crafts. Booths manned by local clubs and residents will also offer other special foods.

Country music is played continuously both days. The Festival will feature Country and Western artist "Lionel Cartwright" on Sunday at 1:00 and 3:00 PM. Also featured will be clogging, kiddie and carnival rides, hot dogs, ice cream, popcorn, pies, soft drinks, coffee, iced tea and cold beer served in Festival mugs that the purchaser gets to keep as souvenirs of his visit to our event.

Madison has campgrounds and motels for guests who would like to spend the weekend. There are many other attractions in Madison and the surrounding areas: swimming, fishing, camping, hiking, horseback rides, boat tours, glider and plane rides, an observation tower to climb and shopping at the town's many fine antique stores. In addition, there will also be a gigantic flea market with bargains galore. Visitors are welcome to set up a table of their own. The registration fee for the flea market is $10 per table.

For those planning to come by plane, the City has an airport with a 2400-foot runway. There is no charge for landing your plane. Volunteers handle plane parking. There is also an area close to the Festival at which arrivals in RVs may park for overnight stays for a modest fee.

EXERCISE 3: **Rewriting News Releases**

INSTRUCTIONS: This is an actual news release. Only the locations and the names have been changed. Your instructor might ask you to write only the lead or to write the entire story. Use the name of your community as the source of the release. The exercise contains numerous errors in style, spelling and punctuation. Use correct indentations, spacing and format.

Why Shield Your Children From Dirty Air When Driving? . . . And How Best to Do It

YOUR TOWN, STATE, TODAY'S DATE—Though air pollution is still a serious threat to public health, it appears to be even more so to the health of our children, recent studies show. Outdoors, indoors, and even while being driven with the windows rolled up, children are potentially more susceptible to the ill affects of pollution than adults.

The news, though, is not all bad. Many motorists may not be aware that most vehicles (2000 and newer) are now equipped with cabin air filters that are designed to clean the air inside the car while you drive.

"However, if this filter is clogged, the dangers from pollutants trapped inside the vehicle can actually multiply," said Polly Ann Georgeson, spokesperson for Hamilton Filters, a leading supplier of automotive filters to the North American aftermarket. (*www.HamiltonFilters.com*) The name of the cabin car filter is No-Worry Filter.

According to Georgieson, even with the windows rolled up and the heating/AC turned on, the air inside can be polluted—if the cabin air filter is not clean.

The American Lung Association's State of the Air Report for 2010 says, air pollution 'shapes how kids' lungs develop.' (www.stateoftheair.org/2010/facts/)

The Clean Air Council (www.cleanair.org), a Pennsylvania-based environmental advocacy group, says that children are more vulnerable to air pollution. They are also more likely to being driven in vehicles, potentially adding to their exposure. Pollutants such as fine dust, deisel soot and nitrogen oxides enter the vehicle through the vents and concentrations of these toxic substances inside can be higher than at the side of the road—all this when children's immune systems are not developed enough to resist the toxins they encounter.

No-Worry Filters offer two types of automotive air filters—the standard particulate filter that traps all types of airborne particles, and an upgraded filter that also removes unpleasant odours.

The standard filter features a scientifically engineered media formed into a multi-layer design with pleats. This provides more surface area to filter out contaminants. These filters are 'electrostatically charged' to ensure that even minute particulate matter gets traped in the filter media.

The upgraded No-Worry cabin air filter features an activated charcoal filter layer that captures and holds most toxic and foul-smelling gasses, such as ozone, nitrogen oxide, sulfur dioxide and hydrocarbons.

Normally located in the cabin air intake, under the dash or behind the glove box, cabin air filters can be easy to replace. It may take anywhere from ten minutes to an hour to replace a cabin air filter, depending on it's location and the vehicle's design.

No-Worry air cabin filters are available for most newer vehicles and come with illustrated specific instructions for many makes and models. These instructions are also available on the website.

Hamilton recommends replacing a vehicle's cabin air filter every 12K to 18K miles to ensure that you shield yourself and your children from environmental pollutants . . . when driving or stuck in traffic even with the windows rolled up.

Name _____ Class _____ Date _____

EXERCISE 4: Writing News Releases

INSTRUCTIONS: The following information is from an actual news release. Write a news release from the information provided. Remember to use Associated Press style. Use as much information as you think necessary to create an effective release. Add phrases and transitions to make the news release acceptable to editors. List yourself as the contact person for the sponsor of the release, decide on the release date and write a headline.

Woman To Woman Conference

Harmony In Your Life
This coming Saturday
8:00 a.m. to 4:00 p.m.
The Peabody Hotel
$35 per person tax deductible donation
Proceeds to benefit the Palmer Hospital for Children & Women

Tickets:	Rosalie Bledsoe 875-6682
Press Info:	Trish Weaver-Evans 628-5431
Featuring:	DR. RUTH Presenting the luncheon keynote address, nationally known television and radio personality, psychosexual therapist Dr. Ruth Westheimer will discuss current sexual issues and how respect for self—and for others—fosters gratifying sexual relationships.
Topics:	The conference will also include 10 exciting workshops presented by area professionals. Each conference participant will choose three of the following:

*Empowerment!

*The Food Trap—Breaking Its Hidden Control

*The Woman's Balance Beam

*Hello, Exercise! Good-bye Blues!

*Fashions for the Shape You're In

*Cosmetic Surgery—The Choice is Yours!

*Why Does He Do That?

*Our Sexual Selves

*Boredom in the Bedroom

Plus: Door Prizes . . . Exhibits . . . Free Booklets & Resource Information . . . Items For Purchase . . . Discount Coupons . . . Book Sales . . . Delicious Luncheon . . . Community Referral Information . . . Woman of the Year Award . . . Opportunities For Growth, Networking, and Fun!

Sponsors: Doctors Health Care Group
Note: Corporate Tables Available
PruCare/PruCare Plus Call: 875-6682
Palmer Hospital for Children & Women

EXERCISE 5: Writing News Releases

INSTRUCTIONS: The information provided below is from an actual news release mailed to a daily or weekly newspaper. Only the locations and the names of some of the individuals have been changed. Write just a lead for the news release or write an entire story from the information.

THE PSYCHIC ZONE

Beyond the edge of understanding, yet just within the fringe of awareness. . . . Beyond the distant future though before the forgotten past, lies a little-understood territory of the human mind that is known as . . . The Psychic Zone!

Saturday April 23 and Sunday April 24th, THE HILTON INN will become part of The Psychic Zone, as a roving contingent of multi-talented psychics proudly present a Psychic Fair for your entertainment.

Many of the psychics will be available for private consultations. Come in and join us, whether you're serious about psychic phenomena, want to enjoy a FREE MINI SEMINAR, or have a private reading.

FREE MINI SEMINARS will be given at 10 AM, 12 Noon, 3 PM and 5 PM. On Saturday night, at 7:30 PM, there will be a PSYCHIC AWARENESS SEMINAR, teaching you how to Meditate, See Auras, Feel Auras, and learn how to reduce stress. Find out how to use your Psychic Abilities. This is a paid seminar, with the cost of admission set at $9.50 for one and all.

THE PSYCHIC ZONE is in your future, April 23rd and 24th, at THE HILTON INN.

EXERCISE 6: Writing News Releases

INSTRUCTIONS: The information provided below is from an actual news release mailed to a daily or weekly newspaper. Only the locations and the names of some of the individuals have been changed. Write just a lead for the news release or write an entire story from the information.

FIRST COMMUNITY RESPITE CARE WEEKEND

Alzheimer's, the fourth leading cause of death among adults in the U.S., has a profound impact on the entire family, thus leaving the primary care giver in a "high risk" category for stress related illnesses. Any time off, regardless of how little, is essential in helping reduce that stress.

Next week, on Saturday and Sunday, Sand Lake Hospital will offer the area's first "Community Respite Care Weekend," a new concept. Volunteers will offer time and loving care the entire weekend.

The Community Respite Care Project offers rest or relief to those families who are continually caring for an Alzheimer's loved one. This weekend will give those family members the opportunity to have a weekend off to do just as they please while their loved one is safe and in the caring hands of trained volunteers and nursing professionals.

After this weekend's respite, similar respite care will be offered on the first weekend of each month at the Sand Lake Hospital facility. The new program also offers in-home volunteer help and subsidized adult day care.

"Anyone who has an interest in volunteering their time is greatly needed," says Charlotte McFarland. Our program relies solely on volunteer power to staff both the in-home and hospital respite. We realize many people may find this type of volunteerism difficult, however, the devoted people we do have find much personal satisfaction and reward once they see how much they help and the difference they make to these families."

For more information, call Charlotte McFarland, Respite Project Director, at 425–2489.

EXERCISE 7: Writing News Releases

INSTRUCTIONS: The information provided below is from an actual news release mailed to a daily or weekly newspaper. Only the locations and the names of some of the individuals have been changed. Write just a lead for the news release or write an entire story from the information.

Name _____   Class _____   Date _____

BLOOD DONORS NEEDED DURING SUMMER MONTHS

Come roll up your sleeve and give a lifesaving gift to a patient who needs you.

The summer is a time for enjoyment and relaxation, but for many local hospital patients who are ill or injured, the summer won't be so much fun. The Blood Bank asks that you help these patients return to good health by donating blood.

"The community blood supply traditionally decreases during this time of the year because many regular donors are on vacation or busy with other activities,: said Linda Wallenhorst-Zito, director of communications and marketing at the Blood Bank. "However, accidents and emergencies increase during the summer, and many patients wanting elective surgery are forced to postpone it until more blood becomes available."

Any healthy person at least 17 years old may donate and there is no upper age limit. Donors complete a brief medical questionnaire and health screening that many find a good way to regularly monitor such factors as their heart rate and blood pressure.

For additional information, call your local Blood Bank branch. Come help save a life. Someday, someone may save yours.

EXERCISE 8: Writing News Releases

INSTRUCTIONS: The information provided below is from an actual news release mailed to a daily or weekly newspaper. Only the locations and the names of some of the individuals have been changed. Write just a lead for the news release or write an entire story from the information.

31st ANNUAL COMMUNITY ART FESTIVAL BEGINS FALL SEASON

Fall is the time to enjoy art festivals everywhere, and our community's 31st annual Fall Art Festival starts the season off right with a weekend show.

Sponsored by the Jaycees, the festival will be held this Saturday and Sunday. Hours are 10:00 A.M. to 5 P.M. each of the two days.

Enjoy first class original artwork in categories including ceramics, watercolors, oils, sculpture, photography and more. Last year's show exhibited 240 artists and drew about 22,000 visitors during the two-day festival.

Food will be available throughout the weekend, along with entertainment, all set along New York Avenue, between 9th and 12th Streets—a perfect setting to enjoy the fall weather and perhaps find that special painting you've been looking for.

For more art festival information, or for information on accommodations in the city, contact the Convention and Visitors Bureau, Box 2007. Call 847-5000.

EXERCISE 9: Eliminating Puffery

INSTRUCTIONS: Rewrite the following sentences and paragraphs more objectively, eliminating all their puffery.

1. The entry deadline is Friday, March 16th, so hurry and sign up!

2. As a proponent of innovative hiring practices, the company's president has worked diligently to hire older workers, disabled workers and the homeless.

3. The governor has not wasted any time. Today the governor announced the selection of a special blue ribbon search committee for the state's university system. This important group is composed of 12 distinguished members with a broad range of interests and will immediately begin its vital task of seeking a new chancellor to head the system.

4. If you're looking for something a bit out of the ordinary for an evening's entertainment, the Center for Arts is the place to be at 7 p.m. Friday and Saturday and at 2 p.m. Sunday. Director Chris Allen will introduce "Love, Love, Love," an exciting new musical comedy certain to please the entire family—and at the low price of only $9.50 a ticket.

5. Johnson is committed to his work and, while serving as head of the Chamber of Commerce in Houston, succeeded in increasing its membership by 41 percent. His goal when he assumes the presidency of the chamber here next week is to achieve the same type of rapid growth. Johnson has already prepared a detailed plan of action outlining the tasks to be accomplished in the months ahead.

6. The stellar cast includes such renowned performers as Hans Gregory Ashbaker as Rodolfo and Elizabeth Holleque as Mimi. Holleque has become one of America's most sought after sopranos since winning the 2003 Metropolitan Opera National Council Auditions. She thrilled audiences here with her portrayals of Marguerite in Faust last season and is sure to do the same with her rendition of Mimi.

7. County residents have many opportunities to register to vote, and Supervisor of Elections Diedre Morsburger likes to make it as easy as possible for them to do so. Kicking off "Voter Registration Month" in the County on the 1st of next month will be a voter registration drive. There will be no need to travel far, Morsburger says. Deputized personnel from her office will fan out to special booths at every major shopping mall in the county to make it easy for residents to register to vote. Morsberger said she has set as her goal next month the registration of 5,000 new voters.

8. Torey Pines is home to a new community of luxury custom homes with lot sizes starting at 1/2 acre and prices from $300,000. In stark contrast to the surrounding properties, which are built on former farmland, Torey Pines stands out as a forest of extremely tall pines and offers a distinctly different skyline. Built by twelve of the area's most renowned custom builders, Torey Pines homes feature floor plans and elevations that are strikingly individual. Eighteen of the finest luxury models will open for the public's inspection and appreciation at noon this Sunday.

9. Guest conductor Richard Hayman and the Symphony Orchestra will bring all the bright lights and excitement of New York's famous theatre district to the stage of the Carr Performing Arts Centre as they present "Broadway Bound," the final concert of the current series, at 8 p.m. Saturday. One of this country's most sought-after "pops" conductors, Hayman is re-invited, season after season, to conduct leading orchestras across the continent. In his usual exuberant style, he will conduct selections from some of Broadway's most beloved musicals, including South Pacific, The Sound of Music, My Fair Lady, Cabaret, Cats and Les Miserables.

Printed in the USA
CPSIA information can be obtained
at www.ICGtesting.com
BVHW020834300723
667916BV00004B/10